Learning in Cyberspace
A Guide to Assessment Tools for Web-based Instruction
Third Edition

✦✦✦✦✦)(✦✦✦✦✦

THOMAS BUCK

J. Wiley & Son Publishing, Ltd.

**Learning in Cyberspace:
A Guide to Authentic Assessment Tools for Web-Based Instruction**
Third Edition

by Thomas L. Buck, PhD

All rights reserved. No part of this book may be reproduced or transmitted, in any form or by any means, electronic or mechanical, including scanning, photocopying, recording, or by any information storage and retrieval system, without permission in writing from the Publisher, and/or from the Author.

J. Wiley & Son Publishing, Ltd., the WILEY logo, Create Space Publish-on-Demand, the Create Space Publish-on-Demand logo, Lloyd & Tutle Publishing, Ltd., and the Lloyd & Tutle logo are registered trademarks with the United States Patent and Trademark Office. Many of the designations used by manufacturers, service providers and sellers to distinguish their products are claimed as trademarks. Where those designations appear in this book, and the author and publisher, was aware of a trademark claim, the designations have been printed in caps, bold or initial caps.

While every precaution has been taken in the preparation of this book, the publisher and author assume no responsibility for errors or omissions, or for damages resulting from the use of information contained herein.

Copyright © 2014 Thomas Buck

All rights reserved.

ISBN: 1495358518
ISBN-13: 978-1495358517

DEDICATION

Because the study of assessment tools is a necessary and integral part of Web-based education, this book is dedicated to all online learners and teachers everywhere.

CONTENTS

Acknowledgments   i

1 Introduction: Virtual Learning Environments   3
    The Learning Environment
    The Community of Inquiry
    Social Schemas
    Evolution of Virtual Learning Environments
    Modular Learning Formats
    A survey of three popular Virtual Learning Environments
      - Moodle
      - Blackboard
      - Canvas

2 Authentic Assessment: A Framework for Web-based Learning   23
    The Research Behind Web-based Authentic Assessment
    Authentic Learning Environments
    Methods for Web-based Authentic Assessment
    Intro to Rubrics
    Web-based Portfolios

3 Instruction Assessment: Practices for Online Teachers   35
    Curriculum Development: Assessment of Learning Objectives
    Lesson Planning for Online Instruction
    Lesson Planning and Curriculum Mapping
    The Curriculum Mapping Process
    Skills Required of Online Teachers
    Additional Resources for Online Teachers

4 Student Assessment: Rubrics and Authentic Assessment Tools   55
    General Rubrics
    Subject-Specific Rubrics
    Rubric Builders, Generators, and Support
    Assessing Serious Games and Virtual Simulations

Glossary: Words for Literate Online Teachers   83
Annotated Bibliography   113
About the Author   143

ACKNOWLEDGMENTS

I have been fortunate to have many friends who shared time with me despite my eccentricities, and without whom this work would never have been started. Of these my thanks goes to Dr. Thomas Gibbons, Dr. Diana Johnson, Dr. Rick Revoir, David Anstett, Sister Mary Rochefort, Kathy Modin, Donna Kirk and Ted Buck – all "Saints" in my book – many of my ideas in this book originated in discussions with them.

I am also grateful to my colleagues Dr. Njoki Kamau, Dr. Iris Yob, Dr. Sunil Hazari and Dr. Barbara Knudson, their incisive comments on my ideas in past research made me re-think how to present my ideas in this book.

Special appreciation goes to my friend, confidant and never-ending role model Dr. John Haire, who through his enduring sense of direction, thoughtfulness and compassion has always helped me to be positive, keep my toils in perspective and my aces high.

Finally, my thanks especially goes out to my truest friend, and personal Managing Editor, Andrea Novel Buck, who patiently and continuously paid attention to every single word in my text, made supportive contributions and suggestions, and when all was done still said she loved me.

1 INTRODUCTION:
VIRTUAL LEARNING ENVIRONMENTS

Technology is transforming American society and education in many positive ways, but some educators think its greatest contribution will be linking students and teachers even if they are geographically far apart through distance learning.

Traditionally, the terms "e-Learning", "distance education" or "distance learning" have been applied interchangeably by many different researchers to a great variety of programs, providers, audiences, and media. Its hallmarks are the separation of teacher and learner in space and/or time (Perraton, 1988), the discretionary control of learning by the student rather than the distant instructor (Jonassen, 1992), and noncontiguous communication between student and teacher, mediated by print or some form of technology (Keegan, 1996; Garrison and Shale, 1987; Buck, 2004).

Today, political and public interest in distance education is especially high in areas where the student population is widely distributed. Each region has developed its own form of distance education in accordance with local resources, target audience, and philosophy of the organizations which provide the instruction. Many institutions, both public and private, offer courses for self-motivated individuals through independent study programs. Students work on their own, with supplied course materials, print-based media and postal communication, some form of teleconferencing and/or electronic networking, and learner support from tutors and mentors via telephone, E-mail, interactive websites, or virtual learning environments (VLE).

The development of virtual learning environments addresses a plethora of needs ranging from rural school districts or underserved urban school districts, to international school and training programs. Some students may enroll in courses to meet graduation requirements which their own schools are unable to offer; some take advanced placement, foreign language, or vocational classes; some may be homebound, home-schooled or disabled. In many instances, talented or gifted high school students have been selected to attend distance classes because of their high academic ability and capacity for handling independent work. This makes classroom management easier, but it may disenfranchise students who lack discipline or time management skills. The resulting inequity of access then becomes a policy problem, not a technology problem.

Designing and delivering virtual learning environments requires thoughtful analysis and investigation of how to use the medium's potential in conjunction with research based instructional design principles and contextual issues critical to various dimensions of Web-based virtual learning, including pedagogical, technological, interface design, evaluation, management, recourse support, ethical, and institutional (Khan, 2001).

The Learning Environment

Although new advances in technology are rapidly changing the world's Web-based learning environments, and "revolutionizing" ways in which technology can assist in virtual learning, but it is widely acknowledged that technology alone won't achieve the most ideal VLE. What is also required is a shared vision that the learning environment caters to, and gives a genuine representation of the specific cultures and communities involved. So, in effect, it is essential that each learning environment, in combination with the research based instructional design, must apply a distinctive approach to e-Learning and use it, along with other approaches, to reflect and contribute to the different learning communities' identities.

Creating the "right learning environment" has become a common theme in e-Learning, and virtual learning environment design. A study of rural schools and their engagement with e-Learning by Stevens (2005) found that in addition to applying the new technologies, changes to traditional learning environments and approaches needed to be made because the creation of "open" or virtual learning environments effectively broke down barriers of space and distance, and required teachers to work more collaboratively.

Traditional learning environments are defined in terms of *time*, *space* and *place*, but when considering a virtual learning environment the additional dimensions of *interaction*, *control* and *technology* need to be considered (Buck, 2004). According to Piccoli et al (2001), VLEs are by definition open systems that allow for participant interaction, enabling students' greater flexibility and control over their learning by providing opportunities for ongoing and more extensive communication between student and teacher.

Harlow et al (2006) suggest that by introducing technology in the classroom a more flexible learning environment is created, changing the role of the teacher from primarily a lecturer to more of a "facilitator of learning". In this environment, students are able to be more involved in their learning and the assessment of their learning, where the teacher provides guidance and facilitates the student to become more responsible for their own learning, a point noted by Chandra and Lloyd (2008). Piccoli et al (2001) refer to this as *learner control*, where students are able to control the level of instruction: reflective of the more flexible learning environment that Harlow et al identified. From their study of laptop use by teachers, Harlow et al (2008) found that teachers were able to:

> "Select, modify and pace content to meet student needs and interests in a way that is impossible with written texts and whole class presentation. In the process of teaching, students were being guided to take responsibility for their own learning (p. 58)."

In general, studies consistently found that the majority of students, regardless of age, culture or location, are significantly aware of the differences between traditional and e-Learning environments and readily adapted to the additional opportunities to engage in the different spaces the e-Learning environment created for them (Buck, 2004; Chandra & Lloyd, 2008; Harlow et al, 2008).

The Community of Inquiry

The Community of Inquiry (CoI) framework is one of the more widely used and effective virtual learning environments (Garrison & Arbaugh, 2007). Central to this model are three complementary elements that contribute to effective learning activities - cognitive presence, social presence, and teaching presence (see Figure 1-1 and Table 1-1). Learning experience takes place through the educational collaboration that occurs where these three elements intersect. Combined with subject specific instructional design strategies, research suggests that the CoI framework presents educators with a computer conferencing medium that readily supports the interpersonal dimension of collaboration, which is related to social presence (Dubuclet, 2008: Richardson & Ice, 2010).

Collaboration

In the Community of Inquiry model, collaboration is key to successful e-Learning, or more specifically, three aspect of collaboration. First, collaboration as a teaching and learning practice; second, collaboration as a method of interaction between resources and participants; and third, collaboration between communities and institutions to facilitate the provision of e-Learning services and products (Richardson & Ice, 2010)

Collaboration in Teaching and Learning

In e-Learning environments, the importance of collaboration cannot be overstated. According to Condie and Livingstone (2007), collaboration impacts on relationships where power structures are altered as students become less reliant on teachers as their primary support for learning. As students are

Community of Inquiry

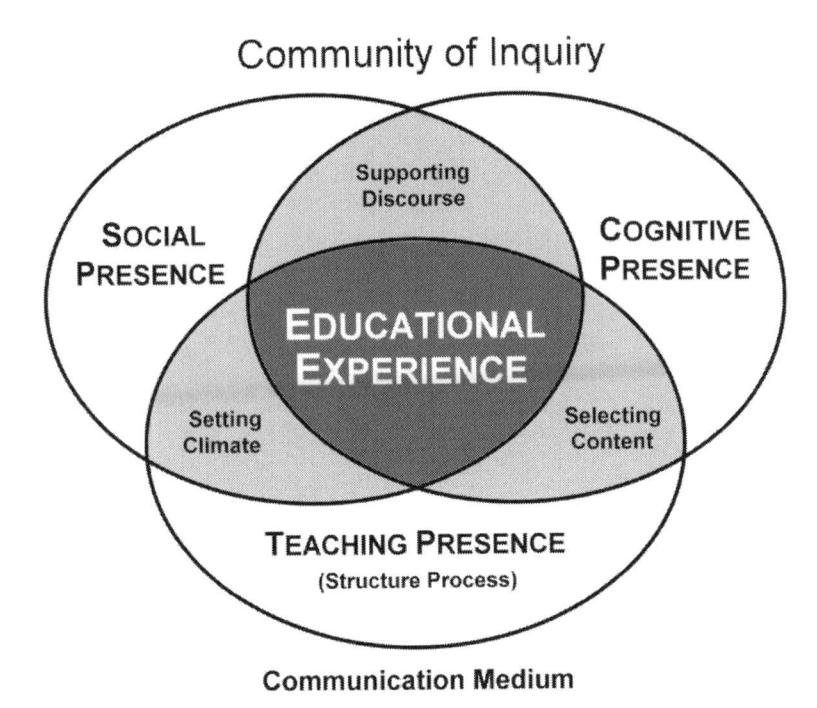

Figure showing three overlapping circles labeled Social Presence, Cognitive Presence, and Teaching Presence (Structure Process), with their intersections labeled Supporting Discourse, Setting Climate, and Selecting Content, and the center labeled Educational Experience. Below: Communication Medium.

Figure 1-1: The basic elements of the Community of Inquiry e-Learning model

encouraged to take on more responsibility for their learning and teachers' roles move more towards facilitation, and represent a fundamental change to the identity of the teacher and the student. This can be an uncomfortable experience, particularly for those holding fast to the 'teacher-expert' model. Such models are deeply embedded and the culture of schools often works against challenging well-established roles and practices.

Elements	Categories	Indicators (examples only)
Cognitive Presence	Triggering Event Exploration Integration Resolution	Sense of Puzzlement Information Exchange Connecting Ideas Apply New Ideas
Social Presence	Emotional Expression Open Communication Group Cohesion	Emotions Risk-free Expressions Encouraging collaboration
Teaching Presence	Instructional Management Building Understanding Direct Instruction	Defining and Initiating Discussion Topics Sharing Personal Meaning Focusing Discussions

Table 1-1: Community of Inquiry Coding Table from Garrison et al. (2000)

Collaboration Between Resources and Participants

Wilson (2004) talks about the importance of collaborative action as a way of ensuring a "custom fit between the static resource and the immediate needs of individuals and groups". He suggests that these actions occur over time, and are influenced by who participates in the process and how the resources are molded to suit the dynamics, purpose and functions of each individual/group action.

In addition, studies have found that as the e-teachers grow in confidence and their knowledge of e-Learning in the CoI expands, they become more adept at assessing the suitability and appropriateness of resources for use in online classrooms (Waiti, 2005). It should be noted however, as Gilbert et al (2007) highlight, there is still a lack of understanding about quality standards for these e-Learning resources.

Social Schemas

Although technology has improved dramatically over the last 20 years to better support collaborative online teaching and learning, many of the social principles remain consistent with the more traditional face-to-face instruction. An instructor needs to let students know about expectations for their work, participation and collaboration, as well as the instructor's availability and approach to feedback. Appropriate online instructional strategies should also be identified and employed in order to create a friendly, communicative and productive online environment for students.

An important issue of collaborative distance education design is the development of lesson plan activities promoting social interactions. This element of VLE course development is perhaps the most nebulous and the most difficult to define. Often accepted as a given in the traditional classroom, the social schema of a course promotes student interaction with the instructor and with other learners. Common VLE activities to promote social interaction include initial ice-breaking and bond building exercises in which students introduce themselves and exchange pictures and names to become familiar with one another. This includes establishing clear guidelines for questions and answers that encourage students at different sites to answer one another during discussions, and allowing students forums or discussion boards for informal talk, especially about shared experiences. In a VLE, these recommendations may mean structuring assignments so students can discuss their personal experiences both as learners and as private individuals. Activities, which build a social bond as well as expect students to interact with the content, include assignments which require students to work in groups to summarize required reading and activities which require students to work in more interactive collaborative environments.

Evolution of Virtual Learning Environments

Virtual learning environments have evolved through the years giving rise to three different types of solutions: (i) open source platforms, (ii) commercial software, and (iii) internally developed platforms.

Open source e-Learning platforms can be customized and adapted by the user and are usually free of a license fee. Most of these applications originally were developed by universities and educational consortiums and are frequently updated and improved by their users. Although commercial e-Learning software packages usually offer additional services, differences between both types of platforms are each time smaller and smaller. Some of the most popular virtual learning environments, such as Moodle, Dukes, Claroline, ILIAS, dotLRN or Canvas belong to this group (see Table 1-2).

VLE & URL	Description
CLAROLINE (http://www.claroline.net)	Initiated in 2001 by the Catholic University of Louvain (Belgium). The software has been translated into 35 languages and is currently used by more than 1700 organizations from 101 countries.
DOKEOS (http://www.8okeos.com)	This e-Learning software is currently used by almost 300 universities around the world, and there are more than 250,000 active Dokeos e-courses at present. It is available in 334 languages.
dotLRN (http://dotlrn.org)	The .LRN software is an e-Learning system developed at the Massachusetts Institute of Technology (MIT) in 2006. It is currently used by more than 500.000 users.
ILIAS (http://www.ilias.de)	Tithe ILIAS learning management system was developed between 1997 and 2000 at the University of Cologne. It is available in more than 20 languages and the user can choose among different interfaces and styles.
MOODLE (http://mooodle.org)	Moodle was originally developed by Martin Dougiamas in Australia in 1999. Currently, it is the most used VLE throughout the world, with more than 2 million users. By December 2010, Moodle had a user-base of 39,868,035 users in 4,180,694 courses in more than 200 countries and in more than 70 languages.
CANVAS (http://Canvasproject.org)	The earliest version of Canvas was originally developed at the Michigan and Indiana Universities. At present, the Canvas Foundation is constituted by more than 100 international universities, colleges and commercial affiliates.

Table 1-2 Open source Virtual Learning Environments (VLE)

Commercial VLE software packages require the payment of an annual license fee for their use. Software providers usually offer technical assistance and some specific modules that improve the functionality of the platform, i.e. whiteboards, advanced course calendars, different kinds of assessment questionnaires, etc. Blackboard, Saba, and e-College are some of the commercial VLE that can be included in this category.

Finally, a great number of specific VLEs have been internally developed by research groups and educational institutions in order to meet the needs off a particular educational model. Nevertheless, many of them are being replaced at present by generic open-source software.

Modular Learning Formats

A popular, and well researched instructional format is the modular learning format. Demetriou (1998) defines modular learning as domain-specific learning. In any modular learning environment, the particular "domains" in the environment affect the functioning of the corresponding domain-specific units, or modules. According to Demetriou (1998), "domain-specific learning" refers to changes in the knowledge structures, processes, and skills within a module in order to better represent or cope with the elements and relations involved in the domain to which this module is affiliated. This type of learning does not generalize; in the Modular Learning Format (MLF) the curricular topic is divided into specific subject areas, rather than broad general classifications (Hart & Rowley, 1996; Demetriou, 1998; Buck, 2004).

Theoretically, the major benefits of a modular curriculum for distance learning is that it provides flexibility in the way programs are constructed and presented. Depending on the curriculum, such flexibility opens up possibilities for students to more closely pursue the depth of a specific topic, set their own pace, more directly influence their learning environment, and decide on the modules to make up their own programs (Hart & Rowley, 1987). In other words, a Web-based MLF allows the learner to select the content and sequence of their educational experience, as well as the time and location. Coupled with this increased flexibility, however, comes greater learner responsibility for navigating through the available choices, and staying on task. This is a significant issue given that various learning styles and cognitive mindstyles are known to differ in their dependency upon and use of navigational and contextual cues, and reading strategies.

Table 1-2 on the previous page is modeled after a modular construct as described by Demetriou (1998). Notice that in the diagram the modular sub-units have external links attached. Among other things, the links could be to optional pages comprised of questions, answers, or related external course

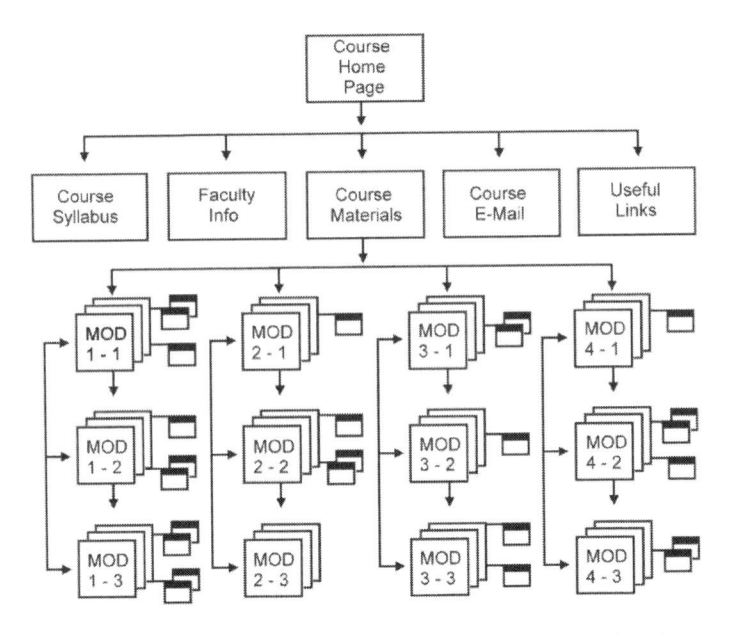

Figure 1-2: Outline of a Modular Learning Environment (MLE).

material. In general, it is expected that students will move through the modular course sections in a more-or-less linear fashion. In addition, the option is always available for them, at any time, to omit a section that they already know, return to a previous module, or to move to a section for which the student has an immediate interest or need (Demetriou, 1998). When constructing a non-linear distance learning environment, with the intent of catering to diverse learning styles, maximizing the options for students is essential.

The work of researchers and theorists including Papert, Brown et al., CTGV, and Perkins have contributed especially important guidelines on how to develop instructional activities according to constructivist models. Because modular instruction systems use a constructivist approach to learning, each of the following principles is considered characteristic of both constructivist purposes, as well as Web-based modular course designs:

Problem-oriented activities – Most constructivist models focus on students solving problems, either in a specific content area such as mathematics or using an interdisciplinary approach; for example, such a problem might require a combination of mathematics, science, and language arts skills. Jungck (1991) says that constructivist methods frequently combine problem posing and problem solving. These kinds of problems are usually more complex than those associated with traditional instruction, and they require students to devote more time and more diverse skills to solve them.

Visual formats and mental models – CTGV is especially concerned that instructional activities help students build good "mental models" of problems to be solved. They feel that teachers can promote this work most effectively by posing problems in visual (as opposed to written) formats. These researchers say that "Visual formats allow students to develop their own pattern recognition skills," and they are "dynamic, rich, and spatial" (1990). This degree of visual support is felt to be particularly important for non-traditional students who may have little expertise or direct guidance in the area in which the problems are posed.

"Rich" environments – Many constructivist approaches seem to call for what Perkins (1991) terms "richer learning environments" in contrast to the "minimalist" classroom environment that usually relies primarily on the teacher, a textbook, and prepared materials like worksheets. Perkins observes that many constructivist models are facilitated by combinations of five kinds of resources: information banks (e.g., textbooks and electronic encyclopedias) to get access to required information; symbol pads (e.g., notebooks and laptop computers) to support learners' short-term memories; phenomenaria (e.g., a computer simulation) to allow exploration; and task managers (e.g., teachers and electronic tutors such as CAI/CMI systems) to provide assistance and feedback as students complete tasks.

Learning through exploration – All constructivist approaches call for some flexibility in achieving desired goals. Most stress exploration rather than merely "getting the right answer," also known as discovery learning. Constructivists differ among themselves, however, about how much assistance and guidance a teacher should offer. Only a few constructivists seem to feel that students should have complete freedom and unlimited time to discover the knowledge they need (Perkins, 1991).

Authentic Assessment Strategies – Constructivist learning environments exhibit more qualitative assessment strategies than quantitative ones. Some popular assessment methods center on student portfolios with examples of students' work and products they have developed (Bateson, 1994; Young, 1995), and performance-based assessments in combination with checklists of criteria (units, modules, exams, etc.) for judging students' performance (Linn, 1994).

A Survey of Three Popular Virtual Learning Environments

To help decide which current VLEs to compare, a review of the most cited VLEs on the Internet was done. The popularity parameter was measured from the number of entrances in two different Web search engines, Google and Yahoo. They were chosen because they are the most popular Web search engines at the moment.

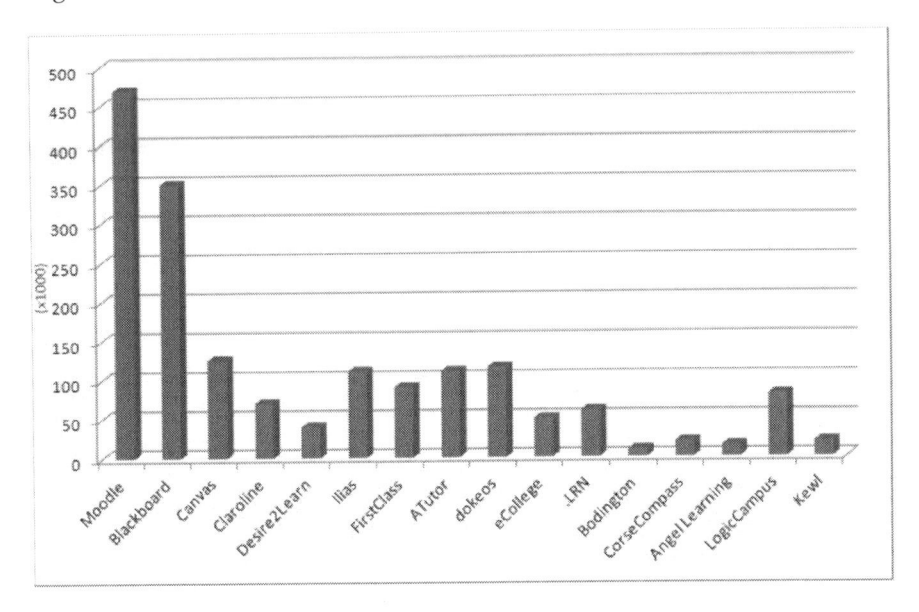

Figure 1-3: The average number of VLE citations on Yahoo and Google search engines over a four week period.

As seen in Figure 1-2, according to Yahoo and to Google, the most prominent platforms are Moodle, in first place, Blackboard in second place, and Canvas, in third place. Because the specific scores change daily, these are the average number of hits over the course of a four week period.

Moodle

Moodle is a course management system (CMS); a free package designed using known pedagogical principles to help the educators to create effective online learning communities, and is an active and evolving work in progress. The word Moodle was originally an acronym for Modular Object-Oriented Dynamic Learning Environment.

LEARNING IN CYBERSPACE

Main Characteristics of MOODLE	
Pedagogy: (Student Centered / Social Constructivist)	The philosophy of Moodle includes a constructivist and social constructionist approach to education, emphasizing that learners (and not just teachers) can contribute to the educational experience. Using these pedagogical principles, Moodle provides a flexible environment for learning communities.
Format (Online / Face-to-Face)	Suitable for 100% online classes as well as supplementing face-to-face learning.
Interface (Simple, lightweight, efficient, compatible, low-tech)	
Installation (Easy to install on almost any platform that supports PHP)	You will need a working Web server, a database and have PHP configured. Specifically, Moodle requires a number of PHP extensions. However, Moodle checks early in the installation process and you can fix the problem and re-start the install script if any are missing.
Compatibility & Support (http://www.moodle.org)	Full database abstraction supports all major brands of database (except for initial table definition). Currently, it is the most used VLE throughout the world, with more than 2 million users. By December 2010, Moodle had a user-base of 39,868,035 users in 4,180,694 courses in more than 200 countries and in more than 70 languages.
Security	Emphasis on strong security throughout. Forms are all checked, data validated, cookies encrypted etc.

Table 1-3 Overview of the open source Moodle Learning Environment

Moodle is provided freely as Open Source software under the GNU Public License. This means Moodle is copyrighted, but you are allowed to copy, use and modify Moodle provided that you agree to: provide the source to others, not modify or remove the original license and copyrights, and apply this same license to any derivative work.

Main Components and Tools of Moodle

Communication	News Forum:	The News Forum is a unique forum that acts as an announcements tool for the Moodle course. It appears by default in the top section of the course homepage and is related to the Latest News block.
	Chat	This function allows real-time, written conversations with other course participants concurrently connected.
	Forums/Discussions	Instructors and students can communicate and collaborate on Moodle using Forums, sometimes called "discussions."
	Mail	The Quickmail block allows instructors, TAs and students, if the instructor allows) to send emails to course members from Moodle. Instructors who use Moodle may find Quickmail a convenient alternative to setting up a class Email list.
Content	Settings Block	The overall settings for the course are found in the Settings block of the main course page. This feature allows teachers to view and/or edit site properties and participants, as well as post articles, assignments, videos, course descriptions, recent announcements, discussion, and chat items.
	Blogs – MoodleDocs	Keep a chronological Web log of news, commentary or events on your site.
	Calendar	Teachers can use this function to post due dates for assignments and tests.
	Activities	Activities are interactive tools used to engage students in learning and asses their progress. Moodle includes the standard tools you'd expect from any learning management system including Forums, Assignments, and Quizzes, along with collaborative activities such as Wiki, Glossary and Database...
	Grading & Tracking	Depending on the teacher's or professor's instructional goals and preferred work process, Moodle provides a variety of options for managing grades during the semester and entering final grades into its management system.

Table 1-4 Basic functions of the Moodle Learning Environment

Moodle can be installed on any computer that can run PHP, and can support a SQL type database (e.g. MySQL). It can run on Windows and Mac operating systems and many distributions of Linux (e.g. Red Hat or Debian GNU). There are many Moodle Partners to assist you, even to host your Moodle site.

Blackboard

Blackboard is an online proprietary virtual learning environment system which is sold to colleges and other institutions and is used on many campuses for e-Learning. Instructors can add to their courses tools such as discussion boards, mail systems and live chat, along with content such as documents and webpages.

Blackboard Inc. was founded by CEO Michael Chasen and chairman Matthew Pittinsky in 1997 and became a public company in 2004. In February 2006, Blackboard Inc. acquired WebCT, a VLE originally developed at the University of British Columbia by a faculty member in computer science, Murray W. Goldberg. As part of the merger terms with Blackboard, the WebCT name was phased out over time in favor of the Blackboard brand. WebCT was notable for being the first commercially successful virtual learning environment (Kolowich 2011).

It had long been criticized for being the most difficult of the course management systems to use. This criticism partly reflected the flexibility and power of the system - where other systems present a single way of organizing or adding course material, Blackboard offers several options with more of the structure left to the individual instructor. Blackboard develops and licenses software applications and related services to over 2200 education institutions in more than 60 countries.

Though Blackboard software is closed source, the company provides an open architecture, called Building Blocks, which can be used to extend the functionality of Blackboard products. The Blackboard Vista and Campus Edition products are extensible through a technology called PowerLinks.

The Blackboard Learning Suite consists of a course management system, a community and portal system, and a content management system. Basic functions are divided into two general categories, Communication and Content (see Table 1-5).

In general, users can move between learning platforms throughout Blackboard with no loss of access to their personal data. The learning platform also accommodates both instructor and student through a changeable functionality designed to meet the needs of the user (Kolowich 2011).

\multicolumn{3}{c	}{**Main Components and Tools of Blackboard**}
Communication	Announcements:	Professors and teachers may post announcements for students to read. These can be found under the announcement tab, or can be made to pop-up when a student accesses Blackboard..
	Chat	This function allows those students who are online to chat in real time with other students in their class section.
	Discussions	This feature allows students and professors to create a discussion thread and reply to ones already created.
	Mail	Blackboard mail allows students and teachers to send mail to one another. This feature supports mass e-mailing to students in a course.
Content	Course Content	This feature allows teachers to post articles, assignments, videos etc.
	Calendar	Teachers can use this function to post due dates for assignments and tests.
	Learning Modules	This feature is often used for strictly online classes. It allows professors to post different lessons for students to access.
	Assessments	This tab allows teachers to post quizzes and exams and allows students to access them via the Internet
	Assignments	This features allows assignments to be posted and students to submit assignments online.
	Grade Book	Teachers and professors may post grades on Blackboard for students to view.
	Media Library	Videos and other media may be posted under this function.

Table 1-5 Basic functions of the Blackboard Learning Suite

LEARNING IN CYBERSPACE

Main Characteristics of Blackboard

Pedagogy: (Student Centered / Social Constructivist)	Promotes collaboration, activities, critical reflection, etc.; designed to caters to instructor planning, diagnosis of learner needs and interests, cooperative learning climate, sequential activities for achieving the objectives, formulation of learning objectives based on the diagnosed needs and interests.
Format (Online / Face-to-Face)	Suitable for 100% online classes as well as supplementing face-to-face learning.
Interface (Functional, menu driven, customizable, compatible, high-tech)	
Installation (Easy to install on almost any platform that supports PHP)	You will need a working Web server, a database and have PHP configured. The LAMS2-Blackboard integration was developed in 2013 with Blackboard Version 7.3 and has been tested 7.x, 8. It is recommended that LAMS and Blackboard be installed on separate servers to account for the heavy memory requirements of Blackboard and LAMS.
Compatibility & Support (http://help.blackboard.com)	Blackboard supports IMS Learning Tools Interoperability (LTI) specifications, making the platform available to institutions using any learning management system (LMS) compliant with LTI industry standards. All functions will be accessible from within the LMS without having to log into more than one system. Blackboard also has announced integration to the open-source Moodle LMS. Blackboard Collaborate's Web conferencing, enterprise instant messaging, and voice authoring capabilities are compatible with Moodle as well.
Security (http://www.blackboard.com)	Blackboard security issues fall under two general categories: (1) scanning technologies and (2) users generated issues. In 2012 Blackboard listed four kinds of security attacks it's next release (Blackboard Learn, Release 9.1 Service Pack 10) will remedy: • Injection attacks • Cross-site scripting • Insecure Direct Object Reference • Cross-site request forgery

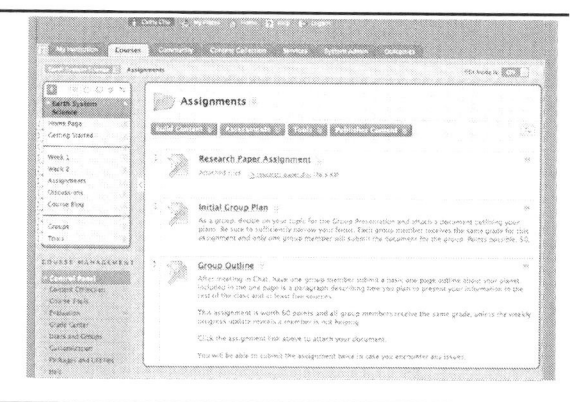

Table 1-6 Overview of the closed source Blackboard Suite

Canvas

Canvas has a clean, intuitive user interface, featuring drag and drop usability; and a comprehensive grading tool. Canvas also allows faculty and students to configure their notification options to integrate with services such as Facebook, Twitter, text messaging and more.

Main Characteristics of Canvas	
Pedagogy: (Student Centered / Social Constructivist)	Unlike Moodle & Blackboard, Canvas is more of a one-size-fits-all solution. Promotes collaboration, activities, critical reflection, etc.; designed to caters to instructor planning, diagnosis of learner needs and interests, cooperative learning climate, sequential activities for achieving the objectives, formulation of learning objectives based on the diagnosed needs and interests.
Format (Online / Face-to-Face / Mobile)	Suitable for 100% online classes as well as supplementing face-to-face learning.
Interface (Functional, both menu driven & drag-n-drop, customizable, compatible, high-tech)	
Installation (Easy to install on almost any platform that supports PHP)	Installing the Canvas Demo involves only a few steps. The most technically challenging aspect of a demo install is making sure that your Java environment is compatible with Canvas.
Compatibility & Support (https://canvas.instructure.com/)	Canvas brings together a variety of integrated technologies, which strongly supports standards-based design and development principles. It is supported on both Mac (OS 10.6 – 10.8) and PC (XP – Win8, and Linux) operating systems, as well as iPad, iPhone and Android.
Security (https://canvas.instructure.com/)	Emphasis on strong security throughout. Forms are all checked, data validated, cookies encrypted etc. At present, Canvas's security is trusted by more than 100 international universities, colleges and commercial affiliates.

Table 1-7 Overview of the open source Canvas Learning Environment

Main Components and Tools of Canvas

Communication	Announcements:	The Canvas software has several options for announcements among teachers and students, reader news RSS, distribution teaching content, to do exams, management of works, etc.
	Chat	This function allows real-time, written conversations with other course participants concurrently connected.
	Forums/Discussions	This feature allows students and professors to create a discussion thread and reply to ones already created.
	Mail	Canvas mail allows students and teachers to send mail to one another. This feature supports mass emailing to students in a course.
Content	Course Dashboard	This feature allows teachers to post articles, assignments, videos, course descriptions, recent announcements, discussion, and chat items.
	Blogger	Keep a chronological Web log of news, commentary or events on your site.
	Calendar	Teachers can use this function to post due dates for assignments and tests.
	Learning Modules	This feature is often used for strictly online classes. It allows professors to post different lessons for students to access.
	Assessments	This tab allows teachers to post quizzes and exams and allows students to access them via the Internet
	Lessons / Assignments	This features allows the teacher to view and post sequenced coursework and assignments and students to submit assignments online.
	Grade Book	Teachers and professors may post grades for students to view.
	Site Editor / Site Setup	Site Editor (instructors only) allows teacher to view and/or edit site properties and participants. Site Setup (My Workspace) lets the student manage properties of their Workspace area.

Table 1-8 Basic functions of the Canvas Learning Environment

The Canvas learning management system (LMS) was founded in 2008 by two BYU graduate students, Brian Whitmer and Devlin Daley,[2] with initial funding from Mozy founder Josh Coates (currently the CEO) and Epic Ventures.

The aim of the Canvas Project is to create a collaborative learning environment for both K-12 and higher education, to compete with its similar commercials platforms (Blackboard), or to improve on open source solutions like Moodle.

Canvas was built using Ruby on Rails as the web application framework backed by a PostgreSQL database. It incorporates JQuery, HTML5, and CSS3 to provide a modern user interface. OAuth is used to provide limited access to a user's information on certain social media sites like Facebook and Twitter to allow for collaboration between sites. Canvas operates as a software as a service using Amazon Web Services in the "Cloud".

Using a Web browser, users can choose among several tools of Canvas to create a place of work appropriated to do courses, projects and research collaboration. In order to do a course, Canvas offers features to support and stimulate education and learning. To carry out mobile and team projects, Canvas has several tools to organize the communication and collaboration work in the campus and around the world.

The Canvas community is actively developing new Canvas tools: IMS Common Cartridge, SCORM, blog tool, shared whiteboard, shared display, multipoint audio, pod-casting, IMS Tool Interoperability, and others.

A Technical Comparison of Platforms

For this part, a comparative matrix of functionality was developed; the end result was that for the most part, the three systems offer largely comparable teaching and learning tools, with major variations in capability. Where significant gaps exist currently, such as Blackboard's inability to provide individual discussion post scores, it is anticipated that these features may change in the near future.

In short, Blackboard offers an integrated suite of products that provide synchronous communication and sharing, collaboration, identity management, and mobile device access, Blackboard does not allow clients to modify the underlying application source code, instead, it relies on feature and enhancement requests. Moodle has a list of features similar to any commercial platform, its user community has also developed a comprehensive list of modules and plug-ins that can be installed or modified to fill the particular needs of any campus; Canvas includes all of the features common to the other two VLEs, but also is intended as a collaboration tool for research and group projects.

In Table 1-9, the features in Blackboard, Moodle and Canvas are compared. Generally speaking, Moodle and Canvas stack up well against Blackboard, and

Major Features Comparison			
Feature	**Blackboard**	**Moodle**	**Canvas**
Upload and Share Documents	Yes	Yes	Yes
Create Content Online in HTML	No	Yes	Yes
Online Discussions	Yes	Yes	Yes
Grade Discussion Participation	No	Yes	Yes
Online Chat	Yes	Yes	Yes
Student Peer Review	No	Yes	Yes
Online Quizzes & Surveys	Yes	Yes	Yes
Online Gradebook	Yes	Yes	Yes
Student Submission of Documents	Yes	Yes	Yes
Self-Assessment of Documents	No	Yes	Yes
Student Workgroups	Yes	Yes	Yes
Student Journals	No	Yes	No
Embedded Glossary	No	Yes	Yes

Table 1-9 Comparison of Major Functions of the examined Learning Environments

when compared side-by-side, it becomes obvious that Moodle and Canvas already have all of the major features of the commercial system Blackboard, as well as a few that it doesn't.

Conclusions

Virtual learning environments are the future in the academic field, not only in higher education, but also at secondary level, where they are being introduced for hybrid as well as fully online courses. They are all used by universities around the world and every day new applications are added to the virtual learning platforms. The objective is to improve the efficiency and the interaction between the students.

In review, all evaluated systems offered some degree of flexibility in terms of supported programming languages. Blackboard is written in Java, and as mentioned earlier, does not allow clients to modify the underlying application source code, relying instead on feature and enhancement requests. The hosted versions of Moodle, which is written in PHP, and Canvas, written in Java, allow for feature enhancements and alterations from their respective service providers. But, as such, end customers cannot make modifications to this code. If Moodle was hosted locally by an institution, access to the entire source code would be possible for full customization. Regardless of whether a commercial or open source environment is ultimately provisioned for school use, version control and issues of "mass customization" vs. a uniform, stable environment for all users will continue to be a topic of discussion.

Of the three, the most used virtual learning environment platform, and the one that has the widest variety of features is Moodle. Its systems have the basic tools necessary for most educational systems, and can be modified and enhanced to meet the changing demands on VLEs.

Regardless, when adopting a system for use, the platform should be selected in terms of its functionality, scalability, and alignment with established online pedagogy of the institution. Cost, while obviously an area of concern for all campuses, should not be the primary factor in system selection.

Key Concepts Discussed
1. **Virtual Learning Environment** (VLE) is an e-learning education system that models conventional education by providing virtual access to classes, class content, tests, homework, grades, assessments, and other external resources.
2. **The Community of Inquiry** is broadly defined as any group of individuals involved in a process of empirical or conceptual inquiry into problematic situations. The community of inquiry emphasizes that knowledge is necessarily embedded within a social context and, thus, requires inter-subjective agreement among those involved in the process of inquiry.
3. **Social Schemas** are social structures or frameworks for organizing and perceiving new information, and can have a direct influence on attention and the absorption of new knowledge:
4. **Modular Learning** is an approach that subdivides a subject or course into smaller parts (modules) that can be studied independently, or as part of a sequence, and then used in conjunction with other units to provide a dynamic and flexible course design.

2 Authentic Assessment: A Framework for Web-Based Learning

The research behind Web-Based Authentic Assessment

As a result of educational and technological advancements in distance learning, instructors and institutions are looking for improved ways to apply authentic assessment into their online courses. In a move to meet some of these needs, Elliot (1995), Winking (1997), Simonson et al. (2000), Boyd-Batstone (2004), Mueller (2011), and Whitlock and Nanavati (2013), among others, created or adapted research-based systems for applying authentic assessment approaches to virtual learning environments.

According to Simonson et al. (2000), in addition to the more traditional cognitive assessment tools (multiple-choice tests, true/false tests, short answers, and essays), two of the primary approaches in authentic assessment are performance assessment and portfolio assessment.

Elliott (1995) describes the major concepts for performance assessment in terms of response generation and response authenticity. In regards to an authentic response:

"A student's active generation of a response that is observable either directly or indirectly via a permanent product. The nature of the task and context in which the assessment occurs is relevant and represents real world problems or issues" (Elliott, 1995).

As was stated earlier, the fundamental goal of authentic assessment is to relate the instruction to the 'real-world' experience of the learners; in other words, for the task to be authentic it needs to have meaning for the learner. Research also suggests that the role of authentic assessments require higher order thinking skills necessary for students to solve real life problems (Bailey, 1998; Winking, 1997).

Elliot (1995) also defined the following points necessary for instructors to increase the effectiveness of performance assessment:

1. Selecting assessment tasks that are clearly aligned or connected to what has been taught.

2. Sharing the scoring criteria for the assessment task with students prior to working on the task.
3. Providing students with clear statements of standards and/or several models of acceptable performances before they attempt a task.
4. Encouraging students to complete self-assessments of their performances.
5. Interpreting students' performances by comparing them to standards that are developmentally appropriate, as well as to other students' performances.

Jon Mueller, creator of the "Authentic Assessment Toolbox" website, points out that most people who discuss authentic assessment do so by comparing it to traditional assessment. Mueller (2011) defines traditional assessment as being "forced-choice measures of multiple-choice tests, fill-in-the-blanks, true-false, matching and the like that have been and remain so common in education. These tests may be standardized or teacher-created (IBID)." According to Mueller, "traditional assessments…can effectively determine whether or not students have acquired a body of knowledge (Mueller, 2011)." In Web-based learning, the goal of using authentic assessment is not to create an antithesis for traditional assessment, but instead to create more of a synthesis of traditional and performance based assessment tools. As Mueller tells us, "it is likely that some mix of the two will best meet your needs (IBID)."

Arguably, the educational theorist Benjamin Bloom made one of the most convincing cases for combining both traditional assessment and authentic assessment tools in Web-based instruction. The following diagram explains Bloom's framework for objectives and assessment in understanding higher-order thinking skills, a fundamental component of authentic assessment.

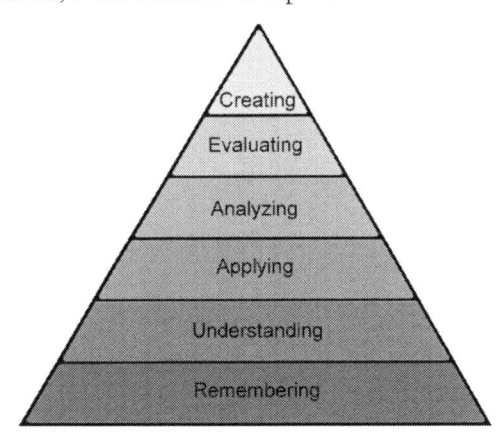

Figure 2-1: The six levels of Cognitive Domain from Bloom's Taxonomy (Anderson & Krathwohl, 2010).

In 1956 Benjamin Bloom and David Krathwohl published a taxonomy of educational objectives (see Fig. 2-1), in which they categorized objectives from simple to complex, or from concrete (factual) to abstract (conceptual), the primary components of what is often referred to as Bloom's taxonomy (Anderson & Krathwohl, 2010), in ascending order are:

1. **Remembering** (*or Knowledge*) – As with authentic assessment, this is the lowest level of objectives in Bloom's hierarchy; it refers to memorization of such things as math facts, historical dates, or verb conjugations.
2. **Understanding** (*or Comprehension*) – Found in both the taxonomy and authentic tools, the need for understanding of information and the ability to use it is a primary component. Examples would include inferring principle of an experiment, interpreting meanings of graphs, or predicting an outcome.
3. **Applying** (*or Application*) – This component relates to the use of knowledge, principles or abstractions to solve real-life problems. The objectives of Application require students to use standards or information to solve practical problems like figuring out how many marbles of a certain size can fit in a box of particular dimensions or using the knowledge of the relationship between temperature and pressure to explain why automobile tires require different air pressures at different times of the year.
4. **Analyzing** (*or Analysis*) – Refers to the breaking down of complex information or ideas into simpler parts to understand how the various parts are organized or relate to each other. Analysis objectives involve having students use the basic or underlying structures of complex facts or thoughts, like understanding how the functions of the software and hardware are related in a computer, or identifying the main plot in a short story.
5. **Evaluating** (*or Evaluation*) – Basically, Evaluation objectives require judging something against a given standard. Students might be asked to appraise or critique a chosen plan of action in a project, or to judge their own work against a set of pre-existing academic or industry standards.
6. **Creating** (*or Synthesis*) – The Creating objective, or highest level goal, is nearly identical in both Bloom's taxonomy and the authentic assessment system. In both, this objective involves creating a new product or solving a problem, by using skills and putting together information in a way that requires original, creative thinking. A good example of this would be for the design of a research project to solve a problem.

In the context of traditional and authentic assessment, the primary importance of Bloom's taxonomy is in its reminder that students need to be reviewed on many levels, from memorizing facts to problem solving in real-life situations. To put this into perspective, the following chart compares and contrasts 15 key points of traditional assessment and authentic assessment tools (adapted from Waterbury Public Schools in Connecticut, 2011).

A 15 Key Point Comparison

Point	Traditional Assessment	Authentic Assessment
1.	Typically limited to tests	Methods and tools include observation, interaction, peer & self-assessment, portfolios, rubrics, etc.
2.	Teacher over and apart from students	Teacher with students
3.	Focus on single subject or topic	Multidimensional and/or multidisciplinary focus
4.	Narrow and specific	Broad and holistic
5.	An event separate from the teaching and learning process	Merged with all phases of the teaching and learning process
6.	Usually occurs at the end of instruction for grading purposes	Occurs during all phases of the teaching and learning process
7.	Teacher-student interaction inappropriate and discouraged during assessment	Teacher-student interaction appropriate and encouraged during assessment
8.	Results in a final number or grade	Results multidimensional (difficult to reduce to a single grade or number)
9.	Assessment restricted to responses to instrument	Teacher can probe and clarify student knowledge
10.	Evaluation primarily conducted by teacher	Encourages self and peer evaluation
11.	Data collection constrained by instrumentation	Flexible and rich data collection
12.	Emphasis on objectivity	Emphasis on flexibility
13.	Concerned with validity, reliability, generalization	Concerned with credibility and transferability
14.	Tasks designed to assess in-school knowledge and/or performance	Connected to and selected from real world tasks
15.	Typically administered on a group basis	Typically administered on an individual basis

Table 2-1 Key point comparison of Traditional and Authentic assessment tools.

It should be noted that compared to traditional tests, authentic tasks are significantly more time-consuming, and reporting or validity can be subjective unless assessment strategies, such as observation forms or rubrics, are closely followed.

By combining these two approaches, the teacher has a much clearer picture of where the learner's knowledge base is; through traditional tests the teacher will get an objective snapshot of what specific knowledge has been acquired at a specific time, and through an authentic assessment, the instructor will be able to track learner's true understanding of that knowledge over a longer period of time.

Authentic Learning Environments

An authentic learning environment is the primary factor of every authentic assessment. Research has shown that on average students are more motivated when they are involved in meaningful tasks; without meaning or purpose the task is not authentic (Whitlock & Nanavati, 2013). Authentic learning environments allow students to solve real life problems by applying newly learned skills and knowledge. The two main components of authentic learning environments are the projects, and the audience. More specifically, the projects can be grouped by the assessment methods they use (see Table 2-2).

Projects – Projects can be created individually or as a group. In order to possess authenticity, they should relate to real life concepts in combination with the learners' prior experience. Any type of activity that displays a student's knowledge about a specific topic (i.e. development of plans, art work, research plans, multimedia presentations, is considered as project. Problem-based learning requires learners to use their problem solving skills to respond to a given situation. For instance, they can be presented a scenario and asked to provide strategies or solutions. The task is assigned to either individuals or groups. They present with the findings they come up with in various forms, such as multimedia presentation, role-play, and written report (Simonson et al., 2000).

As Web-based instruction increases across the board, in all disciplines, the development and application of authentic assessment tools have begun adopting established systemic approaches to, among other things, the grading rubric design. According to Boyd-Batstone (2004) it is important to base your work on specific content standards whenever you are designing authentic assessments.

Audiences – Projects go a step further when students are allowed to present their work to an authentic audience. Web-based learning dovetails perfectly with this aspect of authentic assessment by giving students access to professionals, having discussions boards, and creating learning materials and objects, such as online tutorials or PowerPoint presentations for the class.

Assessment Methods	Authentic Learning Environments — Related Projects
Performance Assessment	Performance assessments test students' ability to use skills in a variety of authentic contexts. They frequently require students to work collaboratively and to apply skills and concepts to solve complex problems. Short- and long-term tasks include such activities as writing, revising, and presenting a report to the class; conducting a week-long science experiment and analyzing the results; or, working with a team to prepare a position in a classroom debate.
Short Investigations	Many teachers use short investigations to assess how well students have mastered basic concepts and skills. Most short investigations begin with a stimulus, like a math problem, political cartoon, map, or excerpt from a primary source. The teacher may ask students to interpret, describe, calculate, explain, or predict.
Open-Response Questions	Open-response questions, like short investigations, present students with a stimulus and ask them to respond. Responses include a brief written or oral answer, a mathematical solution, a drawing, diagram, chart, or graph.
Portfolios	A portfolio documents learning over time. This long-term perspective accounts for student improvement and teaches students the value of self-assessment, editing, and revision. A student portfolio can include: • journal entries and reflective writing • peer reviews • artwork, diagrams, charts, and graphs • group reports • student notes and outlines • rough drafts and polished writing
Peer Assessment	Peer assessment not only distributes the workload of evaluation across the learning environment but also offers students the opportunity to think critically about the process of evaluation itself. Learners might be asked to reach a class consensus on what constitutes satisfactory and exemplary performance on a variety of tasks. They may be presented with evaluation alternatives and asked to weigh the usefulness and limitations of various assessment instruments such as checklists, rating scales, written analysis, and so on.
Self-Assessment	Self-assessment requires students to evaluate their own participation, process, and products. Evaluative questions are the basic tools of self-assessment. Students give written or oral responses to questions like: • What was the most difficult part of this project for you? • What do you think you should do next? • If you could do this task again, what would you do differently? • What did you learn from this project?

Table 2-2 Key point comparison of Traditional and Authentic assessment tools.

Methods for Web-based Authentic Assessment

Authentic assessment methods include open-ended questions, exhibits, demonstrations, hands-on execution of experiments, computer simulations, and portfolios (Whitlock & Nanavati, 2013). The two common alternative assessment techniques, portfolios and projects, are discussed below.

Basically, authentic assessment seeks to match a course's instruction to the real-world experiences of its learners (Boyd-Batstone, 2004). Consequently, authentic assessment methods and strategies dovetail nicely with VLEs, and provide a unique educational opportunity for both distance learning users and providers. In designing a Web-based course, here are some of the more common strategies recommendations for online educators:

Long-term Written Assignments – For long-term written assignments that require the use of materials from an entire semester, the assignment can be broken up into phases that allows the students to submit short-term sections for feedback. Feedback is important but it is labor intensive to prepare. To minimize time usage, develop rubrics ahead of time that students can use to guide them in their work (see Creating Rubrics). Share examples of past students' works, and open opportunities for peer assessment.

Online Discussion Boards – As with written assignments, rubrics can be used to guide student projects on discussion boards. Discussion board rubrics can be as simple as a checklist that specifies target performance criteria for an assignment. Developing the rubric before the beginning of the course can help clarify the objectives of the assignments. Students gain as well, using it as they move through the projects, it can help them understand your expectations and fine tune their performance accordingly. Once you have developed the rubric, it can simplify your grading process. Discussion board rubrics can include specifications for how frequently students should post, how many initial and follow-up posts students are required to make, and the manner in which students are expected to relate postings to course content.

Self-check Quizzes – For courses that teach dense, technical material, self-check quizzes can be very effective to oblige students to complete the required reading and help them (and instructors) gauge their understanding of the material. Most CMS platforms incorporate a mechanism for deploying such quizzes; instructors can experiment to see what features are available. Many platforms offer multiple options for generating automated feedback either immediately after a student completes the quiz or at a later time/date.

Synchronous Technologies – Real-time conferencing is key in helping "close the gap" that asynchronous communication introduces. In fact, Brandy Whitlock, and others (2013) strongly recommend using synchronous technologies, whenever available and appropriate. Realistically speaking though, not all students in an online class will be able to attend a virtual conference session at the same time each week, given that one of the major reasons students enroll in online courses is the convenience and flexibility of the asynchronous format. Recording the sessions for the students who cannot attend Student presentations may be done via web conferencing at the end of the semester. Taking advantage of synchronous technologies may create some of those "incidental opportunities" for learning that instructors say they miss (Whitlock & Nanavati, 2013).

Intro to Rubrics

As will be discussed further in Chapters 3 and 4, authentic assessment rubrics are the foundation for Web-based learning. Defined by the instructors' goals, the rubrics guide the learning experience both in preparation as well as application. Through both peer and self-assessment, the rubric is one authentic assessment tool in which students themselves are directly involved in the assessment process. By design, it is a formative type of assessment tool because it is a dynamic and integral part of the whole authentic teaching and learning process. As was stated earlier, the advantages of using rubrics are that they:

- allow assessment to be more objective and consistent
- focus the teacher to clarify his/her criteria in specific terms
- promote student awareness of the criteria being used
- provide useful feedback regarding the effectiveness of the instruction
- provide benchmarks to measure and document progress

In addition, authentic assessment rubrics blur the lines between teaching, learning, and assessment. As students become familiar with rubrics, they can assist in the rubric design process. This involvement empowers the students and as a result, their learning becomes more focused and self-directed. In this context, rubrics can be created in a variety of forms and levels of complexity, but regardless, they all contain common features which:

- focus on measuring performance, behavior or quality
- use a range to rate performance
- contain specific performance characteristics arranged in levels indicating the degree to which a standard has been met

There are many rubric formats. The grid format shown in the example below (Fig. 2-2) is one of the most common lay outs for a rubric.

Rubric for Asynchronous Discussion Participation

Name_____

Asynchronous discussion enhances learning as you share your ideas, perspectives, and experiences with the class. You develop and refine your thoughts through the writing process, plus broaden your classmates' understanding of the course content. Use the following feedback to improve the quality of your discussion contributions.

Criteria	Unacceptable 0 Points	Acceptable 1 Point	Good 2 Points	Excellent 3 Points
Frequency	Participates not at all.	Participates 1-2 times on the same day.	Participates 3-4 times but postings not distributed throughout week.	Participates 4-5 times throughout the week.
Initial Assignment Posting	Posts no assignment.	Posts adequate assignment with superficial thought and preparation; doesn't address all aspects of the task.	Posts well developed assignment that addresses all aspects of the task; lacks full development of concepts.	Posts well developed assignment that fully addresses and develops all aspects of the task.
Follow-Up Postings	Posts no follow-up responses to others.	Posts shallow contribution to discussion (e.g., agrees or disagrees); does not enrich discussion.	Elaborates on an existing posting with further comment or observation.	Demonstrates analysis of others' posts; extends meaningful discussion by building on previous posts.
Content Contribution	Posts information that is off-topic, incorrect, or irrelevant to discussion.	Repeats but does not add substantive information to the discussion.	Posts information that is factually correct; lacks full development of concept or thought.	Posts factually correct, reflective and substantive contribution; advances discussion.
References & Support	Includes no references or supporting experience.	Uses personal experience, but no references to readings or research.	Incorporates some references from literature and personal experience.	Uses references to literature, readings, or personal experience to support comments.
Clarity & Mechanics	Posts long, unorganized or rude content that may contain multiple errors or may be inappropriate.	Communicates in friendly, courteous and helpful manner with some errors in clarity or mechanics.	Contributes valuable information to discussion with minor clarity or mechanics errors.	Contributes to discussion with clear, concise comments formatted in an easy to read style that is free of grammatical or spelling errors.

Examples of postings that demonstrate higher levels of thinking:
- "Some common themes I see between your experiences and our textbook are...." (analysis)
- "These newer trends are significant if we consider the relationship between...." (synthesis)
- "The body of literature should be assessed by these standards...." (evaluation)

Figure 2-2 An example of a authentic assessment rubric for participation in an asynchronous discussion board (Willis, 2009).

Web-based Portfolios

Traditionally, portfolios consist of student work that displays mastery of skill of the task and expression. Brandy Whitlock, and others (2013) define portfolios as "a purposeful collection of student work that exhibits the student's efforts, progress, and achievements in one or more areas."

Because of their cumulative nature, portfolios require a lot of input from and responsibility of the student. The ongoing cycle of data collection must include student participation in selecting portfolio contents based on individual learning goals, the criteria for the activities' assessments, the group curriculum plans, and evidence of student self reflection.

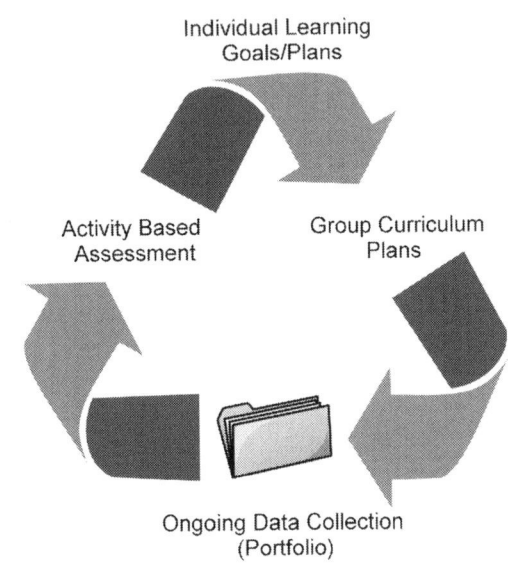

Figure 2-3 A diagram of the portfolio cycle of data collection.

A Web-based, or electronic portfolio (e-portfolio), is a technology-based form of authentic student-based assessment with a collection of work that showcases an individual's skills, abilities, experiences and accomplishments in a meaningful way. One of the primary differences with a Web-based portfolio is that it allows a multi-dimensional, and multimedia focus on student learning (curricular and co-curricular via documents, images, videos and sound), while also allowing for the assessment of learning and later transitions to professional/showcase portfolios. There are several types of e-portfolios, which include:

Archive/Comprehensive: Primarily for the owner's reference, it is a way to store, organize and reflect on personal, professional, and academic work or experiences in a central holistic space.

Course/Learning: A way for a student to store and share assignments for evaluation and feedback as part of an academic course.

Assessment: Primarily to assess competencies as defined by program standards and outcomes. This usually is created by a student, program, or department to demonstrate competencies and skills gained in specific areas of multiple academic requirements.

Professional/Showcase: Created solely for the sharing of professional and academic work with colleagues or prospective employers.

Although the practicality of Web-based or e-portfolio use is highly dependent on the instructor's, as well as the learner's, knowledge of computer and information technology, the benefits include a broader, more in-depth look at what students know and can do; base assessments on more 'authentic' works; and, a richer or better way to review and communicate student progress through online documents (Whitlock & Nanavati, 2013).

Summary

Across the board, Web-based learning environments are being introduced at all levels, for hybrid as well as fully online courses, and the research based implications of Web-based authentic assessment education are far-reaching and positive. Online authentic assessment, in combination with more traditional assessment tools, will allow educators to truly know what their students are capable of.

While the traditional forms of assessment such as standardized tests may continue to give teachers a good snapshot of their students' knowledge of the curriculum, authentic education gives a more true view of not just knowledge, but the students' higher-order thinking skills necessary for them to deal with meaningful tasks in the real world.

More specifically, authentic assessment, when used in conjunction with traditional formats, gives teachers an idea of how well students are able to apply, analyze, synthesize, and evaluate concepts. Skills and knowledge are demonstrated. Some examples of authentic tasks include research projects, writing assignments, giving presentations, portfolios, and solving real-life problems. Most of these assessment models are project-based and research-based. Evaluation includes observation, rubrics and portfolios.

The authentic assessment rubric is a formative type of assessment tool designed to be an integral part of the teaching and learning process. Although rubrics can be designed in a number of styles and levels of detail, they all contain common features which:

- focus on measuring performance, behavior, or quality
- use a range to rate performance
- contain specific performance characteristics arranged in levels indicating the degree to which a standard has been met

By involving students in the creation of the rubric, the students take more responsibility for their own learning, are empowered by being involved in the teaching/learning process, and have a clearer idea of what is expected in terms of specific performance.

Electronic, or Web-based, portfolios can be used to record, display, and monitor student learning process. The types of the authentic assessment portfolios include:

- archive (or comprehensive)
- course (or learning)
- assessment
- professional (or showcase)

As an assessment tool, the benefits of the Web-based portfolio system include a broader, more in-depth look at what students know and can do.

Web-based authentic assessment gives the online instructor a more accurate image of what the students' strengths and challenges are, and what they are able to do with their learned skills and knowledge than do simple tests by applying the concept of evaluating real work into all areas of the Web-based curriculum.

Key Concepts Discussed

1. **Authentic Assessment** is the measurement of "intellectual accomplishments that are worthwhile, significant, and meaningful," (Whitlock & Nanavati, 2013) as compared to standardized tests. When applying authentic assessment to student learning and achievement, a teacher applies criteria related to "construction of knowledge, disciplined inquiry, and the value of achievement beyond the school" (Elliot, 1995).
2. **Authentic Learning** is an example of "backwards learning design" (Whitlock & Nanavati, 2013) because the curriculum follows from the assessment; the framework for learning and assessment begins with the question: "What should students be able to do?" Once the instructor answers that question, they can then devise a rubric to evaluate how well a student demonstrates the ability to complete the task (Simonson et al., 2000).
3. **Rubrics** list expectations of quality around a task, and are primarily used to delineate a consistent criteria for grading. A rubric allows teachers and students alike to evaluate criteria, and can also provide a basis for self-evaluation, reflection, and peer review.
4. **e-Portfolios** are a type of learning record that provides actual evidence of achievement. An e-portfolio is a collection of such things as inputted text, electronic files, images, multimedia, blog entries, and hyperlinks. e-Portfolios are both demonstrations of the user's abilities and platforms for self-expression (Whitlock & Nanavati, 2013).

3 INSTRUCTION ASSESSMENT: PRACTICES FOR ONLINE TEACHERS

Curriculum Development: Assessment of Learning Objectives

Although many of the steps in planning a distance learning course will be familiar to instructors of classroom-based courses, the demands of teaching without face-to-face contact with students make the planning process particularly important.

In curriculum development there is an old saying, instruction and assessment are "two sides of the same coin." Significant changes in one requires changes in the other. The same holds true with curriculum design and assessment; because instruction (or learning) objectives are used in the context of how they will be measured, it is only logical that objectives are an integral part of the authentic assessment process.

Setting out specific course objectives for teaching and learning at the very beginning of the design process is a critical step in developing an online framework for the curriculum. In Web-based authentic learning, an objective could be defined as a statement of skills or concepts that students are expected to know at the end of specifically mapped out points during the course.

	Performance	Conditions	Criterion
	An objective always says what a learner is expected to do.	An objective always describes the conditions under which the performance is to occur.	Whenever possible, an objective describes the criterion of acceptable performance.
QUESTIONS ANSWERED:	What should the learner be able to do?	Under what conditions do you want the learner to be able to do it?	How well must it be done?
EXAMPLE:	"Correctly use adjectives and adverbs."	"Given ten sentences with missing modifiers…"	"…the student will correctly choose an adjective or adverb in at least nine of the ten sentences."

Table 3-1: Parts of an authentic learning objectives statement.

As was stated earlier, online learning objectives are written in such a way as to make clear how the objective will be measured. Regardless of the type of learning involved, or the level of students to whom they are addressed, they all have several things in common. Based on the behavioral objectives developed by Robert Mager (2005), authentic learning objectives have three parts: performance, conditions, and criterion.

As shown in the example (see Table 3-1), in practice, the learning objective framework described would follow this order. First, a statement of the conditions for assessing the learning. The second part describes what skill the student will be able to demonstrate. The third part is a statement of the measure, or criterion, of achievement. Here are some additional examples of learning objectives:

- The student will write a 400 hundred word (minimum) essay describing the ethical dilemma of falsifying financial reports described in the Case Study webpage entitled *Enron's Ethical Dilemma*.
- The student will list at least three possible but creative uses for bulleted lists.

In addition to the obvious advantages of writing and using learning objectives for online teaching, here are some others to consider:

Managing Instruction – In the modular formats of virtual learning environments discussed in Chapter 1, objectives may be used by instructors and students to sort and direct learners and learning activities. They may be used to pre-test students for pre-requisite skills, redirecting to remedial work those who lack the pre-requisites, and skipping ahead those who can demonstrate the skills or knowledge the unit is designed to teach.

Managing Learning – Where managing instruction suggests that the control rests with the instructor, managing learning implies a more active role for the student. Students can use learning objectives to guide their work - choosing necessary tools, collecting research materials, etc. Learning objectives can also be for authentic self-evaluation used in shaping the student's individual learning goals or plans (see Chapter 2, Fig. 2-3).

Planning Instruction – After developing a set of learning objectives for a course you can more logically map the curriculum (as will be discussed later in this chapter), budget time for units, assemble materials, prepare outlines, etc. Objectives also can be used as a guide to teaching, as when you plan different instructional methods based on the desired learning outcomes (e.g., student peer reviews of online reports to give students experience in evaluating content logic and correct usage). A review of course content may result from a look at the learning objectives for the course. After comparing previously used assessment tools with your newly developed learning objectives, you may discover that you need to shift or combine one type with another to which clearly demonstrates the students' mastery of the content, skills, or concepts.

Enhancing Learning – If the student has a set of learning objectives which provide information about their expected e-portfolio content, or a way in which they can demonstrate an acquired knowledge and skill, then the student can make more appropriate choices about the materials and methods for their on-going data collection.

Facilitating Evaluation – Learning objectives can make possible various assessment activities, instructional evaluations, student evaluations, and curriculum reviews. They can form the basis for determining levels of traditional testing to combine with authentic assessment needed to demonstrate a mastery of a skill or goal. They also can be used to demonstrate effective teaching by matching student learning to desired outcomes.

Designing or Redesigning Curriculum – When setting out to improve instruction in a particular course, begin with the content and generate objectives, new materials, etc., based on that content.

- Study of the existing curriculum can draw attention to redundancy and omissions which can lead to curriculum revision.
- Sets of objectives for one course may be compared with the expected entry behaviors for the next course in the sequence. The two should interlock; where they do not, curriculum adjustments can be made.

Producing New Insights – The process of developing learning objectives has one other major benefit, it is said to produce major changes not only in the course, but also in those who take on the job of instructional design. For example, those instructors who spend the time developing learning objectives and mapping the curriculum tend to acquire increased understanding about what is a reachable goal. The writing of objectives also focuses attention away from content and onto the students. This re-focusing often produces revisions in the approaches to teaching and the assessment tools used. In addition, when students are involved in defining the learning goals and plans they become more conscious of the difficulties in defining what it is they want to learn and of choosing from among various objectives.

Lesson Planning for Online Instruction

Writing effective lesson plans for online instruction can be a intimidating task for even the most seasoned teacher. Lesson plan writing for a virtual learning environment is in many ways vastly different from writing lessons for the "real world" classroom, yet the fundamental principles remain the same; there are certain elements that must be included in every lesson plan, online or face-to-face. An effective lesson plan takes thought and preparation, and should meet the particular needs of the students, as well as the instructor's individual style of teaching. It can be broken down into the following three primary components or steps: 1) the Introduction; 2) the Learning Tasks/Developmental Activities; and 3) the Conclusion.

Creating a motivating lesson plan is the first step to having a powerful impact on students. The following sections will discuss the specific parts of an effective lesson plan that you will want to practice as a online teacher.

		Main Components of an Online Lesson Plan (Part 1)
Introduction	Learning Objectives	A statement of skills or concepts that students are expected to know at the end of specifically mapped out points during the course. • Clearly defined • Measurable • Use tools like Bloom's Taxonomy
	Curriculum Objectives	A curriculum objective is a purpose or end stated in specific, measurable terms. From curriculum goals, we derive curriculum objectives.
	Assess Prior Knowledge	Online students will have a broad range of pre-existing knowledge, skills, beliefs, and attitudes, which influence how they attend, interpret and organize in-coming information. Pre-course or introductory activities can help us assess and acknowledge student strengths.

Table 3-2 Outline of the Introduction in a lesson plan.

The Introduction

The introduction to an online instruction lesson plan is the same as the opening sentence of an essay because it draws the student or reader in (see Table 3-2; Fig. 3-1). The introduction of an effective lesson plan will set up the activities to follow. This part of the lesson plan will introduce students to the concepts and goals of the lesson. It will also help students understand how the lesson plan relates to previous lessons and future lessons (Burden & Byrd 2012). Giving students a guideline of what they will gather from the plan will help the class achieve the desired goals.

The Learning Tasks / Developmental Activities

The next step to creating and implementing an effective lesson plan is developmental activities. During this part of the lesson plan teachers should engage the students' interests and stimulate learning through activities. This part of the lesson plan can be completed using several methods such as real-time lectures/PPTs, individual assignments, group assignments, real-time question-answer sessions, and many other means (Burden & Byrd, 2012). This part of a lesson plan is effective when it requires students to interact with the content and coursework. It is important for teachers to consider and accommodate students' learning styles during this part of effective lesson planning (see Table 3-3; Fig. 3-1).

	Main Components of an Online Lesson Plan (Part 2)	
Learning Tasks /Developmental Activities	Teacher-facilitated Lesson	Teacher Facilitated lessons are lessons that can be downloaded from the Internet to your own computer for use in the classroom. These activities offer opportunities for students to learn particular concepts. Although these lessons are facilitated by the teacher to some degree, they must: • Present the material • Demonstrate desired outcome
	Guided Practice	Guided practice is an activity that provides students the opportunity to grasp and development concepts or skills and requires teachers to monitor student progress. Guided practice is not simply assigning a worksheet, problems, or questions to be completed in class.
	Group Activity	Effective online group activities often fall into one of three categories: • There's no right answer, such as debates, or research on controversial issues. • There are multiple perspectives, such as analyzing current events, cultural comparisons, or case studies. • There are too many resources for one person to evaluate, so a jigsaw puzzle approach is needed with each student responsible for one part.
	Closure	Closure is the time when you wrap up a lesson plan and help students organize the information into a meaningful context in their minds. A brief summary or overview is often appropriate.
	Independent Practice	Through Independent Practice, students have a chance to reinforce skills and synthesize their new knowledge by completing a task on their own and away from the teacher's guidance.

Table 3-3 Outline of the Lesson Body / Developmental Activities in a lesson plan.

The Conclusion

During the conclusion of creating an effective lesson plan the teacher must sum up the ideas learned from the lesson. The teacher should also relate this information to future and past coursework to provide students with a broad understanding of the ideas and skills learned. It is important to allow students enough time to ask questions, assert assumptions, and summarize the lesson during this part of the lesson plan (see Table 3-4; Fig. 3-1).

	Main Components of an Online Lesson Plan (Part 3)	
Conclusion	Assessment	Review what was learned against the learning objectives identified at the start of the lesson
	Extension/Follow-up Activity	Indicate how other activities/materials will be used to reinforce and extend this lesson. Include homework, assignments, and projects.

Table 3-4 Outline of the Conclusion / Assessment in a lesson plan.

The process outlined above describes only the main components of an online lesson plan, but does not detail how to effectively deliver the lesson. To help, here are some other aspects to consider:

Multi-Cultural – Make real-world and cross-curricular connections to help students tap into prior knowledge and experiences, thus making learning easier and more relevant to the wider context.

Accommodate Learning Styles – Differentiate instruction in order to accommodate all learners and learning styles. Educators must be able to adjust lessons and activities to meet the needs of all learners in the online classroom, from those with special needs, to high-achieving students, and every learner in between.

Assessment – Check for learning frequently. Whether using a simple real-time question–answer session or learner response devices (Blackboard's Collaboration Tools, Moodle's Realtime Quiz or Canvas's Feedback Loops), the most effective online teachers check for understanding often. Doing this allows for early intervention and review or acceleration of a concept.

Resources – Use the resources available in the classroom or school. When preparing a lesson, talk with a teaching assistant, librarian or technology teacher about what the lesson covers and gain feedback on who can help, and how to create an effective lesson or activity.

Lesson Plan Templates – The variety of templates range from simple fill-in-the-blank forms created by other teachers to more sophisticated Web-based lesson templates with interactive help, state and national standards alignment, collaboration, and more extensive planners. When choosing an online lesson plan format, there are a number of variables that an online teacher must

Learning Objective:					
Learning Tasks / Developmental Activities:					
Conclusion:					
Location(s) Online:					
Time	Image	Script		Student Activities	Media
Low Tech Version:					
Notes:					

Figure 3-1 An example of an Online Lesson Plan template used by the author.

consider, including institution or district guidelines, the virtual learning environment, teaching style, experience and successful practices. The following is a list of generally accepted lesson planning templates.

Online Lesson Plan Forms and Websites	
Madeline Hunter Lesson Plan Template Model (http://www.d.umn.edu/~hrallis/courses/3204sp05/assignments/hunter_lp.html)	The Madeline Hunter Direct Instruction Lesson Plan Model has been the most broadly used lesson plan template for more than 30 years. It is based on her research into effective teachers and the eight essential elements of their lessons at all grade levels.
Understanding by Design Unit Plan Template - Backward Design Process (http://www.d.umn.edu/~hrallis/courses/3204sp05/assignments/ubd_template.htm)	The template for UbD emphasizes beginning with the end in mind -- establishing learning goals for a curriculum unit, and working backwards. The framework was designed by Grant Wiggins and Jay McTighe. It's important to understand that this template is best used for planning a unit. It is not designed to be used as a daily lesson plan template. Think of UbD as the framework from which daily lesson plans and assessments can be designed.
Google Docs Blank Lesson Plan Templates (https://docs.google.com/templates?category=7&q=lesson+plan&sort=user&view=public)	Google Docs has an enormous collection of lesson plan templates and forms created by users. As with other collections, these include individual plans, weekly planners, unit planners, monthly, etc. To help you wade through such a large collection, Google offers helpful sorting tools for highest rated and most frequently used.
Microsoft Office Blank Lesson Plan Templates (http://office.microsoft.com/enus/templates/results.aspx?qu=lesson+plan&ex=1&origin=CT010253063)	Microsoft Office users contributed more than 25 templates and forms to this collection of Microsoft Word and Excel based Lesson Plan Templates. Individual lesson templates, weekly planner templates, unit plan templates, and homeschool templates available in this collection.
LearnBoost Lesson Plan Template and Tools (http://www.learnboost.com/tour)	If you use Google apps for Education or Google Calendar, you'll find the LearnBoost interactive lesson planner particularly useful. It has a weekly planner that can be integrated with your Google calendar. In addition to the template form it has a grade book, and seating chart.
UDL Lesson Builder (http://lessonbuilder.cast.org/)	An interactive Web-based lesson plan template for creating lessons for students of varied learning abilities in the classroom is the Universal Design for Learning (UDL) Lesson Builder from the Center for Applied Special Technology (CAST). The site has several excellent lesson plan samples that illustrate how to construct lessons for differentiated instruction to meet a variety of student needs, skills, and aptitudes. This interactive template provides plenty of guidance and tips for creating a plan.

Table 3-5 Public Online Lesson Plan templates and forms.

Lesson Planning and Curriculum Mapping

Instructors who are new to curriculum mapping may be confused about the difference between lesson plans and curriculum maps. Planning is a design of what we want to teach and mapping is a look at the course we actually taught. In online education, these can be two very different things. To help understand the format and process of mapping, basic templates and skills are described here. The basic differences between lesson planning and curriculum mapping are:

- Planning is organizing content, not mapping.
- Mapping is reporting, not planning.
- Planning is designing the hypothetical (theoretical) curriculum.
- Mapping is revealing the true (operational) curriculum.

Curriculum mapping asks teachers to design the curriculum via authentic examination, collaborative review, and student-centered decision making. It is a calendar-based procedure for collecting and maintaining a database of the operational ("real-time") curriculum in a course, institution or district. Curriculum maps display explicit connections between content, skills, and assessment. The maps are not static but are live, fluid documents that change as teachers revise and improve instruction (Jacobs, 2006).

The Curriculum Mapping Process

The term curriculum mapping is drawn from the work of Heidi Hayes Jacobs (2006), and as stated above is a procedure where the instructors or institution identifies and plans the essential curricular content of a course or program, often referred to as the essential questions (EQ), as seen in Figure 3-2. Then in curriculum mapping, the instructors record exactly what they are doing in their lessons. In general, the information being recorded usually breaks down into at least three specific data fields; content, skills and assessments (Fig. 3-3). The final product is a "map" of the actual curriculum that the students are receiving. This allows the instructor to reflect on both the positive and negative aspects of their course's operational procedures; see if their current curriculum is matching with their lesson plans, as well as the overall mission and vision statements of the school; and, gives them a clear path they may need to fill in any gaps that may be present. The whole process can be better explained in the following four-step approach:

Phase 1: Planning Essential Content – Teachers plan out the content, skills and assessments they intend to use with their students. For a standard template/guide from Tangient LLC (2013), see Figures 3-2 through 3-6.

Phase 2: Curriculum Mapping – Teachers keep an on-going record of the content, skills and assessments they actually use with their students. For a template, see Figures 3-7 and 3-8.

Phase 3: Post Mapping Review – The Curriculum Map findings are compared with the initial lesson plans and curriculum goals in order to discover any potential flaws or gaps. For a template, see Figure 3-9.

Phase 4: Curriculum Map Editing / Revising – Over the course of a predetermined period of time, the changes will be implemented throughout the overall operation of the curriculum.

Curriculum mapping takes time, and teachers need to have a proper understanding of the purpose and overall process, and what is required in order for it to be successful. In addition to standardized templates, curriculum mapping software such as Rubicon (http://www.rubicon.com/AtlasCurriculumMapping.php) and TODCM (http://todcm.org/) are available to help organize the process. Additional online tutorials, templates, forms, programs and services are listed in Table 3-6.

Essentials/Curriculum EQ: How do I know what to teach?		
Understand	*Be able to*	*Know*
➤ That curriculum organization impacts student learning	➤ Find standards appropriate to content/grade ➤ "Chunk" standards ➤ Identify concepts ➤ Create a content map for a unit ➤ "Unpack" standards/ Clarify learning goals ➤ Write an essential question for a unit	➤ What standards are ➤ Why it is important to use standards ➤ How to "chunk" standards ➤ What a concept is ➤ Why it is important to organize instruction around concepts ➤ What an essential question is ➤ Why it is important to use essential questions ➤ What it means to clarify learning goals ("unpack"/"unwrap" standards) ➤ Why it is important to clarify the learning goals ("unpack"/"unwrap" standards) ➤ What a content map is ➤ Why it is important to create a content map
Assessment: "chunking" of QCC/GPS, content map, "unpacked" standards for unit/clarified learning goals, EQ for unit		

Figure 3-2 An outline (part 1) for Planning Essential Content of the Curriculum. Note: EQ = Essential Question; QCC = Quality Classroom Consortium – a group of over 50 school districts, universities, and non-profit organizations (Tangient, 2013).

Evidence/Assessment		
EQ: How will I know they learned it?		
Understand	*Be able to*	*Know*
➢ That the quality of assessment impacts the quality of instruction and learning ➢ That assessment is a critical part of instruction	➢ Design a culminating/authentic assessment for a unit ➢ Create a checklist and rubric for culminating assessment ➢ Create a balanced assessment plan for a unit	➢ What the *Backward Design* is ➢ Why use the *Backward Design* to plan instruction ➢ What authentic/performance assessment is ➢ Why use authentic/performance assessment ➢ What rubrics are ➢ When to use rubrics ➢ When to use checklists ➢ What summative assessment is ➢ What formative assessment is ➢ What a balanced assessment plan includes
Assessment: Authentic culminating assessment, rubric, checklist, a variety of assessments (balance)		

Figure 3-3 An outline (part 2) for Planning Essential Content for Assessment. Note: EQ = Essential Question (Tangient, 2013).

Engagement/Instruction		
EQ: How do I teach so my students learn?		
Understand	*Be able to*	*Know*
➢ That planning and implementing a variety of teaching strategies promotes student engagement and learning	➢ Design appropriate extending & refining lessons for the unit ➢ Design appropriate "acquisition"/"new learning" lessons ➢ Incorporate a variety of teaching strategies into lessons (including cooperative learning, mnemonics, graphic organizers, lecture strategies, questioning strategies, and critical thinking) ➢ Plan differentiation of content, process or product.	➢ What engagement is ➢ What essential questions are ➢ Why EQ's are important ➢ Learning occurs in three levels ➢ Lessons should be planned using the *Backward Design* ➢ Structure of an acquisition lesson ➢ Structure of an extending & refining lesson ➢ Practices that promote student engagement and learning ➢ Why it is important to plan summarizers ➢ A variety of teaching strategies (including: collaborative learning, mnemonics, graphic organizers, lecture strategies, questioning strategies and critical thinking) ➢ Why differentiation is important ➢ What to differentiate ➢ How to differentiate
Assessment: Acquisition/new learning lesson plans, extending & refining/critical thinking lesson plans, differentiation component for unit		

Figure 3-4 An outline (part 3) for Essentials of Instruction (Tangient, 2013).

Environment/Classroom Management
EQ: How do I manage the students and classroom to maximize learning?

Understand	Be able to	Know
- Elements of Effective Classroom Environment
- Strategies for Managing the Classroom
- Various classroom set-ups and how they impact student interactions
- Processes and Procedures for Rituals and Routines
- Strategies for Rapport and Respect with and for students
- Suitable student data to organize in grade book	- Procedures must be practiced again and again until they become routines
- Routines increase student responsibility
- A classroom discipline plan establishes guidelines for expected behavior of students
- Building a professional rapport with students creates an atmosphere of trust, which increases student achievement
- The importance of accurately and consistently organizing student data in grade book	- Create a plan for implementing respect and rapport for all students
- Create a classroom management plan
- Create a plan to develop rituals and routines for classroom
- Develop effective procedures for organizing grade book

Assessment: Plans-Respect and Rapport, Classroom Management, Rituals and Routines, Grade Book

Figure 3-5 An outline (part 4) for Planning Essential Content for Management. Note: EQ = Essential Question (Tangient, 2013).

Enhancement/Professional Responsibilities
EQ: What is expected of me as a professional educator?

Understand	Be able to	Know
- The standards for the Code of Ethics
- The rules for reporting infractions
- The role and responsibilities of the Georgia Professional Standards Commission
- Components for Georgia's Highly Qualified Teacher
- Duties and responsibilities of a teacher
- Professional growth opportunities and responsibilities of an educator	- Educators in Georgia have a governing board that monitors the professional conduct of all educators
- The standards set by the PSC protect the environment for students
- It is the responsibility of every educator to continue to learn in order to provide a quality education for students	- Explain how adherence to our breaking the Code of Ethics (as well as school/ system duties and responsibilities) can effect student learning
- Link professional growth to student learning
- Develop a professional growth plan (IIP)

Figure 3-6 An outline (part 2) for Planning Essential Content for Assessment. Note: EQ = Essential Question (Tangient, 2013).

| Curriculum Map |
| Grade _____ Subject _____ |

Month	Content	Skills	Assessments	Standards

Figure 3-7 A blank Curriculum Mapping template (Buck, 2009).

Curriculum mapping templates are meant to be used with a focus on wording, format and intra-alignment with curriculum design in mind. If not yet implementing curriculum mapping, or just beginning the prologue/planning process, it is recommended viewing/studying samples (such as shown in Fig. 3.8) to help in the systemic map-writing protocols when mapping the curriculum.

Curriculum Map

Grade(s): 11-12 Subject: AP Computer Science

(Semester 1 - Weeks 1-18) Unit / Weeks	Content	Skills	Assessments	Standards
Lesson 1 - Background (Weeks 1-3) - 1.1 History of Computers - 1.2 Computer Hardware and Software - 1.3 Binary Representation and Information and Computer Memory - 1.4 Programming Languages - 1.5 The Software Development Process - 1.6 Basic Concepts of Object-Oriented Programming	Chapter 1 of Textbook *(Fundamentals of Java)* This is the only chapter in the book that is not about the details of writing Java programs. It discusses computing in general, hardware and software, the representation of information in binary (i.e., as 0s and 1s), and general concepts of object-oriented programming. All material is structured to give a broad understanding of computing and a foundation for the study of programming.	To give a brief history of computers. To describe how hardware and software make up computer architecture. To understand the binary representation of data and programs in computers. To discuss the evolution of programming languages. To describe the software development process. To discuss the fundamental concepts of object-oriented programming.	Website Analysis Activity Quizzes from Website – History, Hardware, Memory, Languages, Software, OOP. Completion of Site(s)– Rubric assessment Observation Checklist Rubric Class discussions and observations Chapter 1 Exam (50 Questions: Multiple Choice, True/False, Fill in the Blank and Short Answer)	College Board - AP Computer Science (http://www.collegeboard.com)
Lesson 2 – First Java Programs (Weeks 3-6) - 2.1 Why Java? - 2.2 The Java Virtual Machine and Byte Code - 2.3 Choosing a User	Chapter 2 of Textbook *(Fundamentals of Java)* Programs are written in programming languages, and the language used in this book is Java. This lesson has the student begin programming with a couple of simple Java	To discuss why Java is an important programming language. To explain the Java virtual machine and byte code To choose a user interface style.	Website Analysis Activity Quizzes from Website – Java, comOOP. Completion of 1st Program(s)– Rubric assessment Observation Checklist Rubric	College Board - AP Computer Science (http://www.collegeboard.com)

Figure 3-8 A portion of a map from an AP Computer Science curriculum (Buck, 2010).

Editing the Curriculum Map-Following Grade Level Comparisons

After examining the school's content map for all grades in this subject, write down your observations. These should be used in a discussion to see what changes are to be considered in the planned curriculum for this subject.

Gaps or overlaps when compared with other grade levels or subjects	Assessment questions or concerns	Gaps or overlaps regarding standards	ITBS implications, other questions, concerns and/or new understandings

Figure 3-9 A blank Curriculum Mapping template (Buck, 2009).

Online Curriculum Mapping Templates, Programs & Services

Entrada (http://www.entrada-project.org)	Entrada is an open source Web-based platform and framework created to allow teachers, learners and curriculum managers a simple way of accessing, interacting, and managing the curriculum within their educational environment. Entrada is ideally suited for the health sciences because of its integrated curriculum tagging features and clerkship support; however, it can easily be modified and adapted to almost any professional program.
Knowledge4You (http://www.knowledge4you.com)	Knowledge4You has been a provider of Business Intelligence Solutions and Software/Solution Development for nearly 15 years. The data structure is hierarchical in design, which allows for flexibility in mapping curriculum elements to their respective competencies. Its curriculum mapping feature allows the system to be flexible and customizable for various professional programs with linked objective, activity, and assessment elements.
TODCM (http://todcm.org/)	TODCM (pronounced: tod-kum) is a software framework that helps schools and organizations to implement a curriculum mapping tool according to their own specific requirements. TODCM is based on the user interface concept of the Zurich Mapping System (ZMS) developed by Greg Curtis, Zurich International School.
Rubicon (http://www.rubicon.com/)	Rubicon is the first educational facility dedicated to curriculum mapping. Its definition of mapping: • A system for focused conversation. • An instrument for transparent partnerships. • The hub of all curriculum initiatives. • The central nervous system of curricular discussions.
Collaborative Learning Inc. Curriculum Mapper (http://www.clihome.com/)	Curriculum Mapper 2010 – specifically designed to align curriculum to state and local standards, it is a robust reporting and diagnostic program that uses real-time data to identify specific needs for improving curriculum, instruction, and assessment.
Curriculum Mapping 101 (www.curriculummapping101.com/)	Curriculum Mapping 101 – a comprehensive resource site developed by Janet Hale. Among other things, it includes curriculum mapping connections, templates and forms, tutorials and services.
NYCCurriculum Curriculum Map Templates & Forms (http://nyccurriculum.wikispaces.com/)	These templates and forms can be used in conjunction with the NYC endorsed *Curriculum Essential Document* to support teachers in planning for the school year. Teachers should make decisions as to which template(s) is most effective in supporting their planning for instruction.

Table 3-6 Online Curriculum Mapping resources.

Skills Required of Online Teachers

There are a number of talents and skills that successful online instructors need, and that sets them apart from successful regular classroom teachers. They include having a genuine interest and competence in technology; an ability to converse using a keyboard; enjoyment from coaching students, more than performing for them; and, isn't limited to teaching in only a linear step-by-step fashion.

More specifically, research has highlighted four key traits that are common with successful Web-based instructors (Jacobs, 2010; Burden & Boyd, 2003; Alden, 1998).

Trait 1: Teaching Style – Interaction is the nature of Web-based instruction. The online instructor is primarily a facilitator who helps students progress through the course by steering, advising, questioning, and giving feedback. Although the same strategy may be effective in the regular classroom, face-to-face teachers tend to act as performance aspect of teaching as much as the instruction (Jacobs, 2010). The learned lecturer mentality doesn't make the transition to Web-based instruction as easily as a coach on the sidelines approach does.

Trait 2: Adaptability – Online instructors spend a great deal of time working with and responding to individual students or teams of students. Unlike regular classroom teaching, from the online teacher's perspective asynchronous Web-based instruction tends to be very nonlinear. For example, within a short period of time, the online teacher might be directing one student to an appropriate project in Module 6, then switch to providing feedback to a different student on Module 8, while almost simultaneously advising another student on Module 4. In short, an online instructor must be able to shift gears quickly and easily (Burden & Boyd, 2003).

Trait 3: Aptitude with Written Language – In contrast to the regular classroom, online communication is primarily through text and graphics. Where face-to-face instruction incorporates the teachers skill in the art of speech, the online instructor must be able to express themselves effectively (and quickly) through written language (Jacobs, 2010).

Trait 4: Technological Proficiency – The Web is no place for a technophobic teacher. Instructing and developing Web-based courses requires an instructor who takes pleasure in using advanced technology, and who enjoys always learning new things. An online teacher must be proficient and at ease with using a variety of computer hardware and software (Alden, 1998).

In addition to these four top common traits, there are other necessary capabilities, basic skills and abilities such as the following:

- Proficiency in Web-based virtual learning environments
- Ability to promote interactions with and among students
- Course management skills
- Fluency in strategies of Web-based instruction and assessment
- Ability to create opportunities for authentic learning and instruction
- Capacity to serve more as a facilitator than a lecturer
- A natural curiosity and a love for teaching (and learning)
- A strong belief in the value of authentic Web-based instruction

Additional Resources for Online Teachers

Finally, to help develop a more dynamic knowledge in online education it is recommended that an instructor experience as many varieties of Web-based instruction as possible to see what works for them, and what doesn't. This can be done through courses, workshops, seminars or online tutorials. Following are just a few examples of the many online resources for Web-based instruction. The resources available are virtually limitless.

Social Media
Professional Learning Networks – These professional learning networks are a direct way for instructors to expand their personal and professional development. Communicate with other teachers, search for best practices, find and adapt free lesson plans. Join some of these full-bodied educators' networks to enhance instruction:
- **Classroom 2.0** – Classroom 2.0 is a free, community-supported network focusing on issues surrounding Web 2.0 and social media. (http://www.classroom20.com/)
- **Educator's PLN** – Teacher-based Ning to collaborate with educators from across the country. Ask questions about strategies and resources, share links and videos on a variety of subjects, and be a part of a greater educational conversation. (http://edupln.ning.com/)
- **Claco** – Request an invite to this community to find, build and share resources with teachers across the hall or across the world - Aligned with Common Core. (http://www.claco.com/)

LEARNING IN CYBERSPACE

Learning Objects and Resources

Online Lesson Plans & Learning Objects – Search these websites for quality lesson plans and learning objects to use in your classroom:
- **The NYT Learning Network Blog** – Find relevant and up-to-date lesson plans based on articles and stories from the New York Times. *(http://learning.blogs.nytimes.com/)*
- **Shmoop** – Subscription-based service gives you access to high-quality literature guides, teachers resources, and more. Pay individually for specific lesson plans, or access free resources. *(http://www.shmoop.com/)*
- **Edufy** – Find, share and edit high quality learning activities shared by other teachers with a focus on STEM education. Edufy makes great teaching easier by providing a broad range of activities that can be mixed and matched to build a learning experience to meet every student's learning needs on every topic. *(http://www.edufy.org/)*
- **Edutopia** – Join the conversation or just search for quality lesson plans and instructional strategies on this site. *(http://www.edutopia.org/)*
- **Teaching Central Pinterest** – Search this Pinterest of recommended websites surrounding a variety of educational topics. *(http://pinterest.com/teachingcentral/)*
- **PBS Teachers** – Find classroom resources and strategies sorted by age and subject level. *(http://www.pbslearningmedia.org/)*

Instructional Games – Consider using specially designed games to emphasize course concepts. More and more designers are creating free online instructional games, or platforms for teachers to create their own game specifically for their lessons, like these examples:
- **Jeopardy Labs** – Create your own online "Jeopardy" game, or choose from already created games. *(https://jeopardylabs.com/)*
- **Class Tools.net** – This free site lets teachers create free games, quizzes, activities and diagrams and host them on their own sites. *(http://www.classtools.net/)*
- **Games for Change** – This organization aims to ·leverage entertainment and engagement for social good· by creating and distributing ·social impact games that serve as critical tools in humanitarian and educational efforts. *(http://www.gamesforchange.org/)*

- **ABC YA** – Use this site to find free instructional games modeled from primary grade lessons that are enhanced to provide an interactive way for children to learn.
  (http://www.abcya.com/)
- **A + Click** – Math games for all ages and grades.
  (http://www.aplusclick.com/index.html)
- **Cookie** – This site of educational games for elementary-age students are designed by child experts and educators.
  (http://www.cookie.com/)

Online Textbooks – Consider "remixing" your textbook, choosing free, online resources compiled together for your students. These sites help you collocate resources to make your own textbook, or contribute to free, open-source textbooks created by similar subject-teachers:
- **Boundless** – Boundless markets itself as a free textbook replacement, using open educational content to create their materials.
  (http://www.boundless.com/)
- **CK-12** – CK12 is an open content, web-based collaborative model of customizable, standards-aligned K-12 textbooks. Available online, or for Kindle or iPad.
  (http://www.ck12.org/teacher)

Key Concepts Discussed

1. **Learning Objectives** provide detailed descriptions of what the student will be able to do when the instruction ends. In the context of Web-based learning, they will typically have a number of different components, which range from descriptive data and technology to information about instructional content, practice, and assessment (Mager, 2005).
2. **Lesson Plans** are a teacher's detailed descriptions of course and lesson content, and are developed as a guide for instruction. In Web-based instruction, design varies depending the learning environment, on the preference of the teacher, the subject being covered, and the needs of the student(s). Online instruction lesson plans can be broken down into the following three primary components or steps: 1) the introduction; 2) the learning tasks/developmental activities; and 3) the conclusion (Burden & Byrd 2012).
3. **Curriculum Mapping** is a 'process', not a one-time initiative, for reviewing operational curriculum, and is based largely on the work of Heidi Hayes Jacobs (1997; 2004; 2006; and 2010). Curriculum mapping maintains an on-going record of a courses curriculum by using templates that display key components of the curriculum: content, skills, assessments, and essential questions (Jacobs 2010; Tangient, 2013).
4. **Online Teaching** is usually matched with distance learning and flexible learning, but it can also be used in conjunction with face-to-face teaching, in which case the terms hybrid or blended teaching are commonly used. The online instructor is primarily a facilitator who needs to be flexible, adaptable, have an aptitude with written language, and be technologically proficient (Jacobs, 2010; Burden & Boyd, 2003; Alden, 1998).

4 STUDENT ASSESSMENT: RUBRICS AND OTHER AUTHENTIC ASSESSMENT TOOLS

As stated earlier, authentic assessment is geared toward methods which correspond as closely as possible to real world experience. It was originally developed in the arts and apprenticeship systems, where assessment has always been based on performance. The instructor observes the student in the process of working on something real, provides feedback, monitors the student's use of the feedback, and adjusts instruction and evaluation accordingly. Authentic assessment takes this principle of evaluating real work into all areas of the online curriculum through a step-by-step series of tasks. The following five step process is based on a standardized authentic assessment template designed to be applicable to most forms of education, including face-to-face, online, or hybrid classrooms. While some of the tasks described in this section may seem self-evident, or not required for Web-based instruction, nearly all are necessary to create a valid and effective authentic assessment plan.

Step 1: Describe the Learning Context – The first step in planning a student assessment is to understand the overall learning context. Considering the subject area, difficulty, constraints, student information, and other characteristics of the course or activity will set the frame of reference for all subsequent planning decisions in a student assessment. Use Worksheet A (Fig. 4-1) to help describe the following key points of the learning context:

- **Course characteristics:** Identify characteristics of the course which includes the difficulty level for students, required prerequisites, the discipline of the content, constraints of teaching the course (e.g. quality and quantity of course content, time, resources, etc.) and the relationship of your course to other courses in the department.
- **Student characteristics:** Document the reasons why students are taking the course, demographics, and students expectations.
- **Classroom characteristics:** Consider the characteristics of the classroom, such as: what technological resources will be available, will you have a TA or graduate assistant, what is the design of the class webpage, and other virtual learning environment features.

Worksheet A: Describe Your Learning Context
Course Characteristics
Course title:
Enrollment:
Teaching Constraints:
Required for graduation?   Yes   No   Identify:
Is the course part of a sequence?   Yes   No   Related courses:
Instructional resources available:
Student Characteristics
% Freshmen: Sophomores: Juniors: Seniors: Graduate:
% International:
Top 5 reasons students take the course:
Student expectations for course:
Classroom Characteristics
Teaching tasks (if applicable):
Seating capacity:
Seating configuration:
Available technology:
Other:

Figure 4-1 Worksheet A: Describe Your Learning Context (Buck, 2009).

Step 2: Identify Stakeholders and Their Needs – Explore your goals as the instructor, the department or institution's objectives, and especially the characteristics and needs of the students in order to clearly determine your assessment purpose and learning objectives of the course or activity. In the context of Web-based learning, the stakeholders are the individuals and organizations that will be affected by the results of the assessment and may include those involved in the online instructional framework and those served or affected by the course itself. In relation to student assessments, needs of stakeholders generally reflect the goals of the instructor, and the needs or expectations of the students. Determining stakeholder needs helps to focus the assessment process so that the results are of the greatest utility. Use Worksheet B (Fig. 4-2) to help identify the stakeholder needs. Follow these steps when using the worksheet:

1. Identify any goals that more than one group is likely to have. Use the fourth column to mark these with an "X" because they are probably more important.
2. Rank the questions by their importance. Assign the same rank to similar goals.
3. The top goals will usually develop into the learning objectives of the course.

Group	Needs	X	Rank
School:			
Department:			
Instructor:			
Students:			

Worksheet B: Identifying Stakeholder Needs

Figure 4-2 Worksheet B: Identifying Stakeholder Needs (Buck, 2009).

Step 3: Create the Learning Objectives – Identifying clear objectives for the course or activity helps determine how to conduct the assessment. In authentic instruction, these objectives are statements that describe the knowledge, skills, or behaviors students are expected to be able to demonstrate by the end of a course or activity. As discussed in Chapter 3, when writing student learning objectives for your course, it is helpful to first create general statements about key concepts, topics and principles. From those general statements you can then write specific objectives for class sessions and for testing (see Chapter 3 for specific guidelines to writing learning objectives).

Step 4: Determine How to Use the Results – Determine whether you will use your assessments to informally monitor student work, provide feedback, document progress, or to formally evaluate student knowledge. Decide how frequently you would like to conduct student assessment. Try to identify at least three points: one early in the semester, one midway, and one near the end of the semester. This will help you monitor student progress and make any adjustments that might be necessary. How you use assessments and how frequently you use them will help you determine which assessment method(s) to use.

Step 5: Create an Authentic Assessment Plan – The assessment plan is a detailed description of how to implement the assessment and can be displayed in a separate document or within the course syllabus. The plan should include the following:

- Course learning objectives
- Assessment points
- The assessment method(s)
- Performance criteria for each method

Use the Methods for Web-based Authentic Assessment section of Chapter 2 to help you determine the best assessment method(s) for your course or activity.

General Rubrics

As was discussed in Chapter 2, authentic, performance-based rubrics helps make Web-based learning meaningful to students and encourages them to be creative, innovative and constructive. Rubrics are especially useful when assessing student projects where there is no clear-cut answer or solution as found in traditional standardized exams. In general, there are three basic categories of rubrics for performance assessment (Borich, 2008):

- Checklists
- Rating scales
- Holistic scoring

Each category has advantages, disadvantages and appropriate applications for classrooms.

Checklist Rubrics – Checklist rubrics are not formally defined as scoring guides per se, but are used in evaluating student work on performance, and consist of specific pre-established performance criteria. Basically, they are a list of behaviors or specific steps, which can be marked as Present/Absent,

Complete/Incomplete, Yes/No, etc. In some cases, a teacher will use a checklist to observe the students. In other cases, students use checklists to ensure that they have completed all of the steps and considered all of the possibilities (see Fig. 4-3).

Analytic (Rating Scale) Rubrics – In Web-based instruction, analytic rubrics with rating scales are the most popular for performance assessment (see Fig. 2-2 for example). Rating scales are used when a simple Yes/No or Present/Absent is not adequate for measuring the performance or product. Although these typically include specific point values, the scales might use terms (such as novice, intermediate, and proficient). The following steps are recommended for completing a rubric with a rating scale (Elliott, 1995):

1. Select the performance target (based on your objectives or standards)
2. Define the performance task (outline all expectations)
3. Determine the dimensions that will be assessed. For example, if you are creating a rubric for assessing a research paper, you might evaluate the research, content, mechanics, and style.
4. For each of the dimensions, identify at least three different "degrees" of performance. The more detail you can include, the better. For example, if one dimension is "research" the degrees might include: Exemplary=at least 5 sources; Intermediate=at least 3 sources; and Novice=less than 3 sources.
5. Assign points (numbers) and/or words (e.g., novice, intermediate, proficient) as the scale to evaluate the learning outcomes.
6. Add a column to record the score for each dimension, as well as a row for the total score.
7. Distribute copies of the rubric to students when they begin the task -- that way they will know exactly how they will be assessed.

Holistic Scoring Rubrics – In general, holistic scoring means there is one overall score instead of discrete dimensions. For example, the short response items for FCAT Reading and Mathematics are scored holistically on a 0-2 scale (see Fig. 4-4). The extended responses are scored on a 0-4 scale. Often used for performances, such as dance or music, holistic scales are used when one, overall score is more important than sub-scores for specific categories. Although holistic scales can be easier to create and easier to score, they do not provide the amount of feedback that is possible with a rating scale that includes multiple dimensions (Elliot, 1995).

Student Name:	Date:
___ Has five lines.	___ Has correct capitalization.
___ Tells a funny story.	___ Has correct punctuation.
___ Has correct rhyming pattern.	___ Contains descriptive words.

Figure 4-3 An example of a Checklist Rubric.

Oral Report
(Holistic Rubric)

5 Excellent: The student clearly describes the question studied and provides strong reasons for its importance. Specific information is given to support the conclusions that are drawn and described. The delivery is engaging and sentence structure is consistently correct. Eye contact is made and sustained throughout the presentation. There is strong evidence of preparation, organization, and enthusiasm for the topic. The visual aid is used to make the presentation more effective. Questions from the audience are clearly answered with specific and appropriate information.

4 Very Good: The student described the question studied and provides reasons for its importance. An adequate amount of information is given to support the conclusions that are drawn and described. The delivery and sentence structure are generally correct. There is evidence of preparation, organization, and enthusiasm for the topic. The visual aid is mentioned and used. Questions from the audience are answered clearly.

3 Good: The student describes the question studied and conclusions are stated, but supporting information is not as strong as a 4 or 5. The delivery and sentence structure are generally correct. There is some indication of preparation and organization. The visual aid is mentioned. Questions from the audience are answered.

2 Limited: The student states the question studied, but fails to fully describe it. No conclusions are given to answer the question. The delivery and sentence structure is understandable, but with some errors. Evidence of preparation and organization is lacking. The visual aid may or may not be mentioned. Questions from the audience are answered with only the most basic response.

1 Poor: The student makes a presentation without stating the question or its importance. The topic is unclear and no adequate conclusions are stated. The delivery is difficult to follow. There is no indication of preparation or organization. Questions from the audience receive only the most basic, or no, response.

0 No oral presentation is attempted.

Figure 4-4 An example of a Holistic Scoring Rubric (Borich, 2008).

Subject Specific Rubrics

The intended use of the results defines the choice of whether to use a checklist, a holistic, or an analytic approach to scoring. If an overall score is desired, a checklist or holistic scoring approach would be more desirable. In contrast, if formative feedback is the goal, an analytic or rating scale rubric should be used. That's not to say that one type of rubric is inherently better than the other; the instructor must find a format that works best for their purposes (Montgomery, 2001). Other factors include the time requirements, the nature of the task itself, and the specific performance criteria being observed.

Regardless of which type of rubric is selected, specific performance criteria and observable indicators must be identified. The specific subject or topic being assessed is one of the primary determining factors in the criteria identification. Drafting a subject specific rubric for Web-based assignments may be doubly difficult, especially if the criteria are ambiguous, or if all the guidelines are not clearly defined. To help in shaping the criteria, and to give a visual sampling of the many different formats and styles of rubrics, this section includes examples of rubrics from the following list:

- Comparison/Contrast Essay Rubric
- Creativity Rubric
- Data Analysis Rubric
- Experimental Inquiry Rubric
- Instrumental Music Rubric
- Learning Skills Rubric
- Observation Rubric
- Oral Presentation Rubric
- Reflection Paper Rubric
- Research Paper Rubric

The Comparison/Contrast Essay Rubric

The rubric in Figure 4-5 is for one of the most common distance learning assignment formats, the comparison/contrast essay, in which the student is asked to focus on the ways in which certain things or ideas (usually two of

	Score 4	Score 3	Score 2	Score 1
Audience and Purpose	Clearly attracts audience interest in the comparison-contrast analysis	Adequately attracts audience interest in the comparison-contrast analysis	Provides a reason for the comparison-contrast analysis	Does not provide a reason for a comparison-contrast analysis
Organization	Clearly presents information in a consistent organization best suited to the topic	Presents information using an organization suited to the topic	Chooses an organization not suited to comparison and contrast	Shows a lack of organizational strategy
Elaboration	Elaborates ideas with facts, details, or examples; uses all information for comparison and contrast	Elaborates most ideas with facts, details, or examples; uses most information for comparison and contrast	Does not elaborate all ideas; does not use enough details for comparison and contrast	Does not provide facts or examples to support a comparison and contrast
Use of Language	Demonstrates excellent sentence and vocabulary variety; includes very few mechanical errors	Demonstrates adequate sentence and vocabulary variety; includes few mechanical errors	Demonstrates repetitive use of sentence structure and vocabulary; includes many mechanical errors	Demonstrates poor use of language; generates confusion; includes many mechanical errors

Figure 4-5 An example of a Comparison/Contrast Essay Rubric (Simonson et al., 2011).

of them) are similar to (this is the comparison) and/or different from (this is the contrast) one another. By assigning such essays, the instructor is guiding the student to make connections between texts or ideas, and engage in critical thinking. The higher goal is for the student to reflect on similarities and differences, helping the student gain a deeper understanding of the items being compared, their relationship to each other, and what is most important about them.

	Superior	Adequate	Minimal	Inadequate
Content	The speaker provides a variety of types of content appropriate for the task, such as generalizations, details, examples and various forms of evidence. The speaker adapts the content in a specific way to the listener and situation.	The speaker focuses primarily on relevant content. The speaker sticks to the topic. The speaker adapts the content in a general way to the listener and the situation.	The speaker includes some irrelevant content. The speaker wanders off the topic. The speaker uses words and concepts which are inappropriate for the knowledge and experiences of the listener (e.g., slang, jargon, technical language).	The speaker says practically nothing. The speaker focuses primarily on irrelevant content. The speaker appears to ignore the listener and the situation.
Delivery	The speaker delivers the message in a confident, poised, enthusiastic fashion. The volume and rate varies to add emphasis and interest. Pronunciation and enunciation are very clear. The speaker exhibits very few disfluencies, such as "ahs," "uhms," or "you knows."	The volume is not too low or too loud and the rate is not too fast or too slow. The pronunciation and enunciation are clear. The speaker exhibits few disfluencies, such as "ahs," "uhms," or "you knows."	The volume is too low or too loud and the rate is too fast or too slow. The pronunciation and enunciation are unclear. The speaker exhibits many disfluencies, such as "ahs," "uhms," or "you knows." The listener is distracted by problems in the delivery of the message and has difficulty understanding the words in the message.	The volume is so low and the rate is so fast that you cannot understand most of the message. The pronunciation and enunciation are very unclear. The speaker appears uninterested.
Organization	The message is overtly organized. The speaker helps the listener understand the sequence and relationships of ideas by using organizational aids such as announcing the topic, previewing the organization, using transitions, and summarizing.	The message is organized. The listener has no difficulty understanding the sequence and relationships among the ideas in the message. The ideas in the message can outlined easily.	The organization of the message is mixed up and random. The listener must make some assumptions about the sequence and relationship of ideas.	The message is so disorganized you cannot understand most of the message.
Creativity	Very original presentation of material; captures the audience's attention.	Some originality apparent; good variety and blending of materials / media.	Little or no variation; material presented with little originality or interpretation.	Repetitive with little or no variety; insufficient use of materials / media.
Length of Presentation	Within two minutes of allotted time.	Within four minutes of allotted time.	Within six minutes of allotted time.	Too long or too short; ten or more minutes above or below the allotted time.

Figure 4-6 An example of an Oral Presentation Rubric (Borich, 2008).

The Oral Presentation Rubric

This oral presentation rubric is designed to fit any topic or subject area. The rubric allows teachers to assess students in several key areas of oral presentation. The rubric is designed to be used by the instructor, or given to students ahead of time for self-assessment so that they know and understand what they will be scored on. The oral presentation rubric discusses each of the major areas and how they relate to oral presentation (Borich, 2008).

The Data Analysis Rubric

Another challenging subject to assess through an authentic approach, is that of data analysis. The rubric in Figure 4-7, the Data Analysis Rubric, is a type of holistic rubric designed for assessing students that are taking raw data and suitably entering it into a spreadsheet (data processing). The processed data is then manipulated to add value using features like sort, filter, formula and equations (Churches, 2008).

	Data Processing	Data manipulation	Data Presentation	Data Analysis
1	Students attempt to arrange data into fields. Most Fields are named. Data entered has some inaccuracies. Students show little understanding of data types.	Students make no attempt to manipulate data or manipulation is fundamentally flawed.	Students inconsistently and inappropriately make use labels, highlights, font weight and underline. Students select inappropriate visual methods of presenting data.	Students make no attempt to analyse data or draw conclusions or the analysis is fundamentally flawed. Students make no attempt to links to prior knowledge.
2	Students arrange data into fields. Fields are named. Data entered has some inaccuracies. Students have some understanding data types – continuous and discontinuous.	Students can manipulate data with use of formula or equations or sort or filter. Some errors are present in data manipulation.	Students use labels, highlights, font weight and underline. Students select visual methods of presenting data. Some presentation methods are suitable for the type of data and purpose of presentation and audience.	Students attempts to identify trends to draw conclusions from the data. There are inaccuracies in analysis. Students attempt to make some links to prior knowledge.
3	Students arrange data into fields. Fields are appropriately named. Data entered is mostly accurately. Students recognise data types – continuous and discontinuous – most of the time.	Students can manipulate data using formula or equations. Students can use the filter and sort features. The data manipulation makes analysis possible. Some errors are present in data manipulation.	Students appropriately use labels, highlights, font weight and underline. Students select visual methods of presenting data. The presentation methods are mostly suitable for the type of data and purpose of presentation and audience. The presentation shows trends.	Students identify trends and are able to draw conclusions from the data. There are few inaccuracies in analysis. Students can recognise some errors and inaccuracies in the processed, manipulated and presented data. Students are able to make some links to prior knowledge.
4	Students arrange data into suitable fields. Fields are appropriately named. Data is entered accurately. Students recognise data types – continuous and discontinuous	Students can appropriately manipulate data using suitable formula or equations. Students can appropriately use the filter and sort features. The data manipulation makes analysis possible.	Students appropriately and consistently use labels, highlights, font weight and underline. Students can select suitable visual methods of presenting data. The presentation methods are suitable for the type of data and purpose of presentation and audience. The presentation suitably and accurately shows trends.	Students correctly identify trends and is able to draw suitable accurate conclusions from the data. Students can recognise errors and inaccuracies in the processed, manipulated and presented data and their analysis. Students are able to relate presented data to other knowledge.

Figure 4-7 An example of a Data Analysis Rubric (Churches, 2008).

Scientific Ability	Missing	Inadequate	Needs some improvement	Adequate
1. Is able to identify sources of experimental uncertainty	No attempt is made to identify experimental uncertainties.	An attempt is made to identify experimental uncertainties, but most are missing, described vaguely, or incorrect.	Most experimental uncertainties are correctly identified.	All experimental uncertainties are correctly identified.
2. Is able to evaluate specifically how identified experimental uncertainties may affect the data	No attempt is made to evaluate experimental uncertainties.	An attempt is made to evaluate experimental uncertainties, but most are missing, described vaguely, or incorrect. Or only absolute uncertainties are mentioned. Or the final result does not take the uncertainty into the account.	The final result does take the identified uncertainties into account but is not correctly evaluated.	The experimental uncertainty of the final result is correctly evaluated.
3. Is able to describe how to minimize experimental uncertainty and actually do it	No attempt is made to describe how to minimize experimental uncertainty and no attempt to minimize is present.	A description of how to minimize experimental uncertainty is present, but there is no attempt to actually minimize it.	An attempt is made to minimize the uncertainty in the final result is made but the method is not the most effective.	The uncertainty is minimized in an effective way.
4. Is able to record and represent data in a meaningful way	Data are either absent or incomprehensible.	Some important data are absent or incomprehensible.	All important data are present, but recorded in a way that requires some effort to comprehend.	All important data are present, organized, and recorded clearly.
5. Is able to analyze data appropriately	No attempt is made to analyze the data.	An attempt is made to analyze the data, but it is either seriously flawed or inappropriate.	The analysis is appropriate but it contains minor errors or omissions.	The analysis is appropriate, complete, and correct.

Ability to collect and analyze experimental data

Figure 4-8 An example of an Experimental Inquiry Rubric (Churches, 2008).

The Experimental Inquiry Rubric

This Experimental Inquiry Rubric on the previous page (Fig. 4-8) was developed by Michael Gentile of Rutgers University as an assessment tool to help his students' meet the rigorous standards of scientific inquiry during their collection and analysis of data (Gentile, 2008).

Name _____

Scale: _____ Selection: _____

	5	4	3	2	1
Rhythm - counting, correct duration of sounds and rests in relation to the beat and to each other.					
Notes - correct pitch and fingering, observation of the key signature. Percussion: note reading on bells.					
Articulation - tonguing and slurring, observation of staccato, legato, accents, etc.. Percussion: execution of flams, rolls, etc.					
Tone - sound production, embouchure (mouth position), playing in tune. Percussion: correct grip on sticks.					
Steady Beat - even, appropriate tempo (speed) throughout piece.					
Posture - sitting up straight and using correct hand and head positions.					

5 = Excellent: no errors or irregularities; continue on present course.
4 = Very Good: no more than 3 errors or minor irregularities; practice performing the test at home.
3 = Good: no more than 5 errors, but skills need refinement; pay closer attention to details while practicing.
2 = Fair: skills need significant work; more consistent practice time is needed at home.
1 = Poor: significant problems with skills; daily practice and private lessons may be a solution.

Figure 4-9 An example of Instrumental Music Rubric (Churches, 2008).

The Instrumental Music Rubric

This rubric was developed as part of a session on ensemble assessment held at the January 2002 Florida Music Educators Association In-Service Meeting in Tampa, Florida. The rubric was developed as part of a group activity that was focused on producing a rubric that met the achievement standard levels of the National Music Standards established by the National Association for Music Education: MENC (Asmus, 2002).

Criteria	Needs Improvement	Satisfactory	Good	Excellent
Works Independently	* Needs prompting to begin task. * Is easily distracted.	* Often needs prompting to remain on task. * Is easily distracted but will usually return to task.	* Begins task promptly. * Stays on task with little external prompting.	* Begins task promptly and stays focused without external prompting.
Teamwork	* Does not work well in a group. * May be disruptive and keep others from working.	* Needs encouragement to work in a group. * Tries to work alone. * May only work well with group when student chooses the group.	* Cooperates with other group members. * Remains on task. * Communicates effectively with group.	* Cooperates with other group members. * Keeps group focused and on task. * Communicates well with group and on behalf of the group.
Organization	* Missing pages from notebook or papers stuffed in locker or bag. * Forgets equipment regularly.	* Has a notebook. * Usually puts worksheets etc. into notebook. * Usually brings equipment to class.	* Keeps notebook and other equipment organized. * Brings equipment to class daily.	* Keeps notebook well organized. * Inserts pages and work as soon as they are received. * Brings all equipment and knows where it is.
Work Habits/ Homework	* Needs a lot of direction to get to work. * Does not do homework	* Needs reminders to get work finished. * Sometimes forgets to bring homework back to class. * Does not always do homework.	* Comes to class prepared to work. * Attempts homework and completes where possible.	* Opens book and gets out equipment before class starts. * Attempts and completes homework daily. * Completes extra work for practice or interest.
Initiative	* Must be told to do everything. * Does not complete work or start another page or exercise without much prompting.	* May or may not seek help when required. * Waits for teacher to notice work is done and another task is required	* Seeks help when required. * Looks for next task to do as each one is completed	* Willing to ask for assistance. * Helps other students when the need arises.

Figure 4-10 An example of a Learning Skills Rubric (Ryan, 2004).

The Learning Skills Rubric

This rubric (Fig. 4-10) was included to help instructors to review the relevant learning skills in a Web-based context. It was developed by Dr. Julie Ryan (2004) to help adult learners develop, manage, and understand the learning skills needed to function effectively in the online learning environment.

Scientific Observation Rubric

Attributes	Above Standard	At Standard	Attribute Still A Goal	Attribute Points Earned
Points Possible	(5-4.5)	(4.0-3.5)	(3.0-0)	
Measurements	Consistently made careful measurements taking time to see that the measurements made sense.	Usually made careful measurements taking time to see that the measurements made sense.	Consistently made measurements without care or reflection.	/5
Use of Class Time	Came to class prepared and equipped, made effective use of time; were always on task and actively involved in the project.	Usually came to class prepared and equipped; usually made effective use of time; were usually on task and actively involved in the project.	Came to class unprepared a majority of the time, not using time effectively or staying on task.	/5
Journal	Kept up-to-date, organized, and labeled journal of all measurements, observations, questions, contacts, and progress. Organization and reflection are evident.	Kept up-to-date, organized, and labeled journal of all measurements, observations, questions, contacts, and progress.	Journal is incomplete or missing.	/5
Project Sustainment	Sustained the project with virtually no intervention from teacher; utilized problem-solving skills to implement the technology.	Sustained the project with some intervention from teacher; utilized problem-solving skills to implement the technology.	Project was not sustained or was sustained with considerable help from the teacher.	/5
Team Work	Consistently worked together as a well-coordinated team; divided large task into a number of smaller tasks; smaller tasks were assigned to team members; team members pulled their own share.	Usually worked together as a well-coordinated team; usually divided large task into a number of smaller tasks; smaller tasks were usually assigned to team members; team members pulled their own share.	Team did not work together and effectively split up tasks. Outside intervention was needed to help split up work; team members did not pull their own share.	/5
Communication and Leadership	Project leader was assigned; effectiveness of his/her role was clearly evident by the level of communication and coordination with each other and the teacher.	Project leader was assigned; effectiveness of his/her role was usually evident by the level of communication and coordination with each other and the teacher.	Project leader was not assigned or was not effective as evidenced by the lack of communication and coordination.	/5
Observation Point Total				/30

Figure 4-11 An example of an Observation Rubric (Henderson, 1997).

The Observation Rubric

This observation rubric (Fig. 4-11) was designed to be used an assessment of student understanding of the behavior of sound and light waves in a physics or physical science course. In addition to the obvious physics content, there is the potential for a strong biology connection (Henderson, 1997).

CATEGORY	Unacceptable (Below Standards)	Acceptable (Meets Standards)	Good (Occasionally Exceeds)	Excellent (Exceeds Standards)	SCORE
Introduction	Does not adequately convey topic. Does not describe subtopics to be reviewed. Lacks adequate thesis statement.	Conveys topic, but not key question(s). Describes subtopics to be reviewed. General thesis statement.	Conveys topic and key question(s). Clearly delineates subtopics to be reviewed. General thesis statement.	Strong introduction of topic's key question(s), terms. Clearly delineates subtopics to be reviewed. Specific thesis statement.	5 points
Focus & Sequencing	Little evidence material is logically organized into topic, subtopics or related to topic. Many transitions are unclear or nonexistent.	Most material clearly related to subtopic, main topic. Material may not be organized within subtopics. Attempts to provide variety of transitions	All material clearly related to subtopic, main topic and logically organized within subtopics. Clear, varied transitions linking subtopics, and main topic.	All material clearly related to subtopic, main topic. Strong organization and integration of material within subtopics. Strong transitions linking subtopics, and main topic.	15 points
Support	Few sources supporting thesis. Sources insignificant or unsubstantiated	Sources generally acceptable but not peer-reviewed research (evidence) based	Sources well selected to support thesis with some research in support of thesis.	Strong peer-reviewed research based support for thesis.	15 points
	Does not summarize evidence with	Review of key conclusions. Some integration	Strong review of key conclusions. Strong integration with thesis	Strong review of key conclusions. Strong integration	5 points

Figure 4-12(a) An example of a Research Paper Rubric (Willis, 2009).

The Research Paper Rubric

The Research Paper Rubric displayed in Figure 4-12 was developed by Julie Willis of the Psychology Department at San José State University (2009). In contrast to a reflection paper, a research paper is a formal report that contains an original idea (thesis) and evidence to back up the idea (research).

Conclusion	respect to thesis statement. Does not discuss the impact of researched material on topic.	with thesis statement. Discusses impact of researched material on topic.	statement. Discusses impact of researched material on topic.	with thesis statement. Insightful discussion of impact of the researched material on topic.	20 points
Grammar & Mechanics	Grammatical errors or spelling & punctuation substantially detract from the paper.	Very few grammatical, spelling or punctuation errors interfere with reading the paper.	Grammatical errors or spelling & punctuation are rare and do not detract from the paper.	The paper is free of grammatical errors and spelling & punctuation.	20 points
APA Style & Communication	Errors in APA style detract substantially from the paper. Word choice is informal in tone. Writing is choppy, with many awkward or unclear passages.	Errors in APA style are noticeable. Word choice occasionally informal in tone. Writing has a few awkward or unclear passages.	Rare errors in APA style that do not detract from the paper. Scholarly style. Writing has minimal awkward or unclear passages.	No errors in APA style. Scholarly style. Writing is flowing and easy to follow.	20 points
Citations & References	Reference and citation errors detract significantly from paper.	Two references or citations missing or incorrectly written.	One reference or citations missing or incorrectly written.	All references and citations are correctly written and present.	**Total Points:**

Figure 4-12(b) An example of a Research Paper Rubric (Willis, 2009).

The research paper assignment is one that many students find intimidating, becoming overwhelmed by all the tasks that are involved. This rubric can not only help instructors with the task of grading it, but can lessen the intimidation to students by giving them a concrete overview of the grading requirements, and what criteria is involved for a quality paper (Willis, 2009).

6	5	4
The work is unusually creative. The ideas/materials/methods used are novel, striking, and highly effective. Important ideas/feelings are illuminated or highlighted in sophisticated ways. The creation shows great imagination, insight, style, and daring. The work has an elegant power that derives from clarity about aims and control over intended effects. The creator takes risks in form, style, and/or content. • The problem has been imaginatively re-framed to enable a compelling and powerful solution • Methods/approaches/techniques are used to great effect, without overkill • "less is more" here: there is an elegant simplicity of emphasis and coherence • Rules or conventions may have been broken to create a powerful new statement. • Common materials/ideas have been combined in revealing and clever ways • There is an exquisite blend of the explicit and implicit	The work is highly creative. The ideas/materials/methods used are imaginative and effective. There is attention to detail. A clear and confident voice and style are present. • Novel approaches/moves/directions/ideas/perspectives were used to good effect • There is an effective blend of personal style and technical knowledge • Familiar materials and ideas have been combined in new and imaginative ways • The work provokes a lively audience response	The work is creative. The ideas/materials/methods used are effective. A voice and style are present. • Novel approaches/moves/directions/ideas/perspectives were used to good effect • There are imaginative and personal touches scattered throughout the work • The work keeps the audience mostly engaged • There is a discernible and interesting effect/focus/message/style, with lapses in execution • The work takes some risks in methods/style/content

Figure 4-13(a) An example of a Creativity Rubric (Buck, 2009).

3	The work is somewhat creative. The ideas/materials/methods used show signs of imagination and personal style. • Familiar approaches/routines/moves were used, but with a few new twists • There are places where ideas and techniques are borrowed whole. • Novel ideas or approaches may be present but they seem stuck on, excessive, out of place and/or not integrated effectively in the work • Time-tested recipes and clichés are used even where there is a personal voice – the work is pretty "safe" • The work is a mish-mash of interesting and familiar approaches and effects, but with no coherence OR the work is technically very competent and coherent, without much spark or insight
2	The work is not very creative. The approach is trite and the ideas clichéd, leading to a flat and predictable performance. There is little sense of the creator's touch, voice, or style here. • The work offers little in the way of new approaches/methods/ideas • There is little sign of personal voice, touch, or style • The work suggests that the creator confuses "creative" and "risk-taking" with "shocking in a juvenile way" • There is excessive and incoherent use of different materials, techniques, ideas • The creator may have confused great care and precision
1	The work is uncreative. • The performance re-creates someone else's performance or relies exclusively on the models/algorithms/moves/recipes/templates/directions/materials provided. • The work is predictable throughout, relying almost exclusively on hackneyed approaches; there is no apparent personal touch • The work is timid and lacking in vivid feelings and ideas – so abstract that it has little to say The work is done with care but without direction or insight

Figure 4-12(b) An example of a Creativity Rubric (Buck, 2009).

The Creativity Rubric

The Creativity Rubric (Fig.s 4-13a & b) is a relatively objective holistic approach to dealing with what is too often considered a subjective issue. In online assessment, creative writing is one of the more difficult areas to grade. It is not merely about personal feelings; it's about communicating those feelings to someone who is not you. Basically, creative writing is defined as anything where the purpose is to express thoughts, feelings and emotions rather than to simply convey information (Buck, 2009).

REFLECTION PAPER RUBRIC			
	Exemplary (A)	**Adequate (B)**	**Needs Work (C)**
Organization	Information is very organized with well-constructed paragraphs, use of subheadings, and information is factual and correct.	Information is organized but paragraphs are not well constructed. Information appears factual	The information appears to disorganized and is suspect to being correct and factual
Quality of Information	Information clearly relates to the main topic. Paper includes several supporting details and/or examples	Information clearly relates to the main topic. No details and/or examples or given	Information has little to do with the main topic
Mechanics	No grammatical, spelling or punctuation errors	A few grammatical, spelling, or punctuation errors	Many grammatical, spelling, or punctuation errors
Sources	All sources are accurately documented in the desired format (APA)	All sources are accurately documented, but many are not all are in the desired format (APA)	Sources are not accurately documented

Figure 4-14 An example of a Reflection Paper Rubric (Bober-Michel, 2012).

The Reflection Paper Rubric

The Reflection Paper Rubric below (Fig. 4-14) was designed by Prof. Marcie J. Bober-Michel of San Diego State University (2012). Like creative writing, without a systematic approach, a reflection paper can be difficult to grade because it is not only a summary, but also a reflection what the subject meant to the author; what the author thinks the meaning behind the topic was; or, what affect it had on them and/or on other people, etc. Notice how this rubric objectively focuses on the form, mechanics and organization of the paper rather than on the author's meaning or interpretation (Bober-Michel, 2012).

Online Rubric Generators, Programs & Services

eRubric Assistant (http://emarkingassistant.com/)	eRubric Assistant is a free rubric generator which works on Windows and Macintosh computers. This tool automates the majority of rubric construction via an interactive interface in Word. Criteria are presented in rows and standards or performance levels for each criterion are presented in columns. A toolbar allows the user to show and edit the scores awarded to a given piece of work by highlighting the attained cells within the rubric. There is a demonstration at the eMarking Assistant website.
ForAllRubrics (https://www.forallrubrics.com/)	ForAllRubrics allows teachers to produce, access and share rubrics online. The system can be accessed via Web and mobile devices including iPad. Real-time analyses showing item and class performance are also available.
iSocrates (http:// http://www.isocrates.org/)	iSocrates allows educators to create rubrics, provide feedback comments, and evaluate student performance. The software can also assign scores and produce rubric-based reports. iSocrates allows instructors to generate criteria pull-down menus featuring their most commonly used feedback comments, and to evaluate student performance from both a qualitative and quantitative perspective.
Rubrix (http://rubrix.com/)	Rubrix allows construction of rubrics for any subject. The Web-based rubrics and observation data automatically sync with various portable devices. Evaluations are uploaded, securely archived, and can be shared with selected individuals. A variety of reports are available for management and analysis of data.
Rubistar (http://rubistar.4teachers.org /)	Rubistar is a free tool which allows educators to create rubrics for assessment tasks. Rubrics can be accessed and edited online. It builds on templates in the subject specific areas of Oral Projects, Multimedia, Math, Writing, Products, Reading, Art, Work Skills, Science, and Music.
Rubrics for Teachers (http://www.rubrics4teachers.com)	Hosted by Teacher Planet, Rubrics for Teachers is a huge compilation of ready-made rubrics for a range of subject areas including Generic Rubrics, Listening Rubrics, Participation Rubrics, Rubrics by Subject, Rubrics by Term, and Rubric Tools.
rGrade (http://www.rgrade.com/)	rGrade™ is an electronic performance assessment system. It supports digital portfolios, rubric development, grading and assessment, and progress mapping.

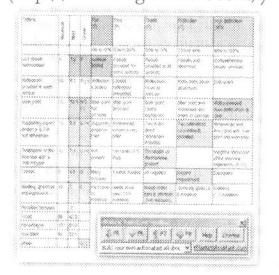

Table 4-1 Online rubric resources.

Online Template Collections & Web 2.0 Rubrics

Required Benchmark Assessments (http://Web.ccsd.k12.wy.us/RBA/RBA.html)	Required Benchmark Assessments is a free K-12 collect of rubric templates for Art, Foreign Language, Language Art, Math, Music, Science, Social Studies, and Wellness.
Rcampus Rubric Gallery (http://www.rcampus.com/rubricshellc.cfm?mode=gallery&sms=publicrub)	Rcampus Rubric Gallery is one of the largest collections of rubric templates, and allows teachers to produce, access and share rubrics online. As of January 2013, the collection (by grade level) included: • K thru 5th – 43334 rubrics • 6th thru 8th – 52509 rubrics • 9th thru 12th – 60929 rubrics • Undergrad – 30941 rubrics • Graduate – 7139 rubrics • Post Graduate – 1205 rubrics
Web 2.0: Twitter Rubrics	Twitter is often used in online education, here are a couple online rubrics to help the instructor consider how they will evaluate the various academic skills that students learn. • Harry G. Tuttle's Twitter in the Classroom (http://eduwithtechn.wordpress.com/2009/06/23/assessing-learning-with-Web-2-0-twitter-in-the-classroom/) • University of Wisconsin – Stout's Twitter Rubric (http://www2.uwstout.edu/content/profdev/rubrics/Twitter_Rubric.html)
Web 2.0: Wiki Rubrics	Wikis have great potential for teaching and learning, here are a couple rubrics for instructors evaluating students using Wiki's in academics. • University of Wisconsin – Stout's Wiki Rubric is designed specifically to be used for assessing individual and group Wiki contributions. (http://www2.uwstout.edu/content/profdev/rubrics/Twitter_Rubric.html) • Wikipedia's examples Wiki Rubrics (http://wikieducator.org/Rubrics/Wiki_Rubrics)
Web 2.0: Blogger Rubrics	Like Twitter, blogs have become common place in online education, below are two rubrics for instructors evaluating students' blog postings. • Clarence Fisher's Blogging Rubric (http://www.evenfromhere.org/2010/02/16/blogging-rubric) • Bowling Green State University's Blogging Rubrics (http://facultydevelopmentbgsu.blogspot.com/2005/11/rubrics-to-evaluate-classroom-blogging.html)
Social Network Rubrics	Twitter, Facebook, Blogger, etc. – Online education regularly uses social networks as a tool for teaching and learning. Here are several useful rubrics for evaluation. • Brad Hachez's Social Net Rubric (http://www.academia.edu/1740757/Social_Net_Rubrics) • 21st Century Skills' Social Networking Rubric (content.cellt.org/diglib/2-18/SocialNetworkingTools_Rubric.pdf) • Social Networking: A Webquest for Educators (edtech2.boisestate.edu/hornyakj/502/Webquest/evaluation.html)

Table 4-2 Online template collections and Web 2.0 rubrics.

Rubric Builders, Generators and Support

On the previous two pages are just a small sampling of the many popular and effective rubric builders and resources on the Internet (Tables 4-1 & 4-2). Included are tools and generators designed to both help and guide the teacher through the process of creating authentic assessment tools for evaluating student performance with Wikis, social networks, blogs and more.

Assessing Serious Games and Virtual Simulations

In closing, there is an additional Web-based learning tool with significant potential that needs to be addressed, that being the assessment of serious games and virtual simulations in online instruction. In the context of education, a serious game, or virtual simulation, is a game designed with a primary purpose other than pure entertainment.

Serious Game Design

- **Learning Game Theory Variables**: Learning, Cognition, Pedagogy, Persuasion, Behavior, Flow-Presence, Pyschology, Gender, Affect
- **Supporting Discourse**
- **Possible Applications**: Cognitive Tutors, Corporate Training, Museums, Health, Social Issues, K-12, Higher Ed, Ecology, Science, All Else
- **Setting Climate & Goals**
- **Serious Games**
- **Selecting Structural Elements**
- **Game Design Category Examples**: 2D/3D Design, World Building, Advergames, Technical Writing, Storytelling, Artificial Intelligence, Programming, Simulations, Fun, Art, Avatars, Level Design

Figure 4-15 Diagram of possible Serious Game Design components.

In Web-based learning, the purpose of a serious game is twofold: (i) to be fun and entertaining, and (ii) to be educational. Consequently, the components of a serious game design must be both attractive and appealing to a broad target audience, similar to commercial games, and meet specific educational goals and applications (see Fig. 4-14). Therefore, to have a valid authentic assessment of a serious game, the aspects of fun/enjoyment and the game's educational impact must be considered.

Distance learning with serious games is primarily a real-world challenge process aimed at clearly defined and measurable achievements standards or goals. Therefore, instructors must implement an authentic or performance based assessment to provide an indication of the learning progress and outcomes to both the learner and instructor (Bente and Breuer, 2009). For serious games to be considered a viable educational tool, they must provide some means of testing and progress tracking, and the testing must be recognizable within the context of the Web-based education or training they are attempting to convey.

Figure 4-16 An example of a serious game, *SimuStar: The Credit Theory Game*, designed for assessing business risk and loan structuring.

Considering the use of serious games in online instruction, Michael and Chen (2005) describe three primary types of assessment: (i) completion assessment, (ii) in-process assessment, and (iii) teacher assessment (see Fig. 4-16). The first two correspond to summative and formative assessments, respectively.

Completion Assessment
Completion assessment is concerned with whether the player successfully completes the game. In a traditional teaching environment, this is equivalent to asking, "Did the student get the right answer?" Although not sufficient to determine whether the player actually learned the material, a simple measure

like this could be the first indicator that the student sufficiently understands the subject taught (Michael & Chen, 2005).

In-process Assessment

In-process assessment examines how, when, and why a player made their choices and can be equivalent to a regular classroom teacher's observations of a student performing a task or taking a test. The serious game's teacher assessment focuses on the instructor's observations and judgments of the student "in action" (while they are playing the game) and typically aims at evaluating those factors that the functionalities/logic of the game are not able to capture. As part of player assessment, especially with multiple players, the instructor can track, monitor and record the players' "in action" activities.

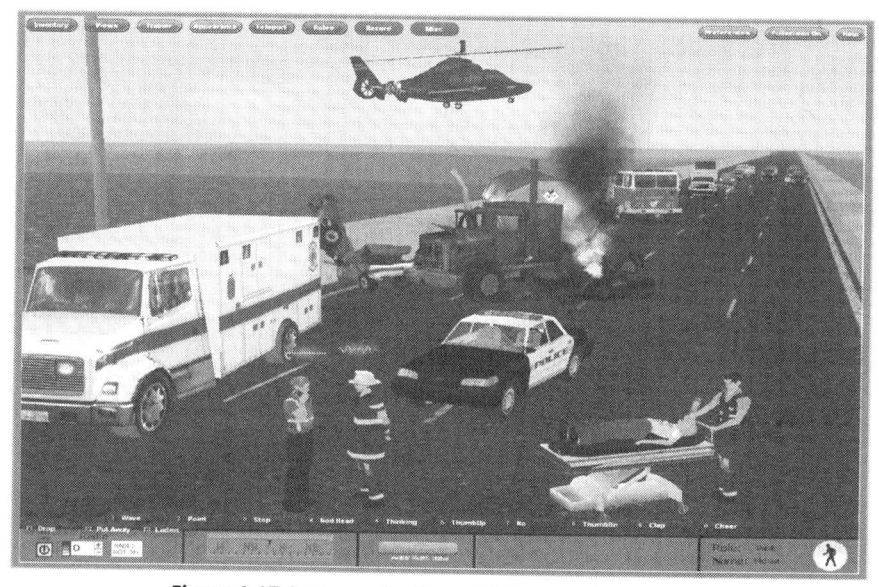

Figure 4-17 An example of a multiplayer serious game, *Safety and Traffic Management.*

Serious games offer logging and tracking potential that has seldom been available or even possible in traditional classrooms. Video games have long had logging features that allow players to replay their performance in the games. Modern games have even begun to learn from the player's actions within the game, adjusting storylines, strategies, monster strength, and other variables to adjust to what the player has done and is doing. Serious games can take advantage of these features. For example, Safety and Traffic Management (see Fig. 4-16) performs detailed logging in its safety simulation software, tracking such data as:

- Time required to complete the lesson
- Number of mistakes made
- Number of self-corrections made

Through the information logged, and the detailed criteria set by the instructor, games like this have almost complete in-process assessment of players, in which the serious game itself determines how well the player is learning. This is especially useful for Web-based assessment on a number of levels, and can be useful with student assessments in modular environments.

Depending on the number of players and the complexity of the game, Juul (2003) suggests that in creating the rubric additional criteria should be taken into account like the players' interaction patterns, roles of the participants, division of labor, community development, the equipment used, etc.

Figure 4-18 An example of a multiplayer serious game, *Masters of the World - Geopolitical Simulator 3*, that can be used in both Secondary as well as Higher Ed.

Another example of a serious game that tracks players' activities is *Masters of the World - Geopolitical Simulator 3*. Used as a political science simulator for both Secondary and Higher Education, and by NATO as an educational tool to train their diplomats, this is considered one of the most realistic geopolitical and world economy simulators to dates. Published in 2013, the game accurate in its portrayal of current world affairs, and let's you take charge of and control any country in the world. It can be played either as a single or multiple user game, and comes with both student and teacher guides.

In developing a rubric for a serious game such as this, a combination of player goals achieved and the "in action" play performed should be considered. The instructor also needs to define an inventory of the games' significant structural elements. Steinkuehler, et al. (2012), identify the six top-level categories of game components as: game aims; game location; game pieces/players; the means of making progress in the game; game language; and the time frames of games. For rubric development, they also summed up the structural elements of into the following list (Steinkuehler, et al., 2012):

- Purpose of the game
- Procedure for action
- Rules governing action
- Number of required participants
- Roles of participants
- Results or pay-offs
- Abilities and skills required for action
- Interaction patterns
- Setting and environmental requirements
- Required equipment

Another aspect of serious games to consider is the specific categorization of the assessment criteria. In making a general rubric for student learning in a serious games, Bell (2008) suggests the following categories (see Fig. 4-18):

- Knowledge of the key aspects
- An understanding of the game rules
- Ability to form game specific problem solving questions
- Ability to identify and apply relevant game information and resources
- Use of creative thinking skills in problem solving.
- Ability to use feedback constructively
- Demonstration of cooperative learning with a group, partner or team

Summary

Rubrics, as with nearly all authentic assessment tools, are geared toward assessment methods which correspond as closely as possible to real world experiences. The instructor observes the student in the process of working on something real, provides feedback, monitors the student's use of the feedback, and adjusts instruction and evaluation accordingly. For authentic assessment of Web-based learning, rubrics are necessary to take this principle of evaluating real work into all areas of the curriculum.

The rubric is a formative type of assessment because it becomes an ongoing part of the whole teaching and learning process. Students themselves are involved in the assessment process, and as students become familiar with rubrics, they can assist in the rubric design process. This involvement empowers the students and as a result, their learning becomes more focused and self-directed. Authentic assessment, therefore, blurs the lines between teaching, learning and assessment.

Game Rubric
Assessing Student Learning in Virtual Simulations and Serious Games

CATEGORY	Exemplary	Proficient	Partially Proficient	Unsatisfactory	POINTS
Knowledge of the key aspects of the simulation or game.	3 points — Identified more than 5 significant aspects in each of the categories of the game (significant events, key characters, division of labor, resources needed, problems to be solved).	2 points — Identified between 5-3 significant aspects in each of the categories of the game.	1 point — Identified less than 3 significant aspects in each of the categories of the game.	0 points — Could not identify any significant aspects of the game.	___/3
Ability to understand and communicate the rules of the game	3 points — Fully articulated all rules and knows where to verify rules.	2 points — Understood the majority of the rules and knows where to find the rules in question.	1 point — Understood a few rules and does not know where to find the rules in question.	0 points — Did not understand the rules of the game nor where to find the rules of the game.	___/3
Ability to construct a variety of question types to help solve game problems	3 points — Correctly constructed at least 5 knowledgeable questions in several different types. For example, closed or multiple choice, true or false, and analytical or evaluative questions.	2 points — Correctly constructed between 3-5 knowledgeable questions in several different types.	1 point — Correctly constructed less than three knowledgeable questions that are the same type.	0 points — Unable to construct knowledgeable questions.	___/3
Ability to locate and select relevant information from a variety of sources to solve game problems	3 points — Located and selected a wide range of relevant information from a variety of sources that will help solve game problems.	2 points — Located and selected relevant information from a few sources that will help solve game problems.	1 point — Located a limited amount of information. Some were not relevant to the game.	0 points — Unable to locate relevant information.	___/3
Use of creative thinking strategies in the game-making or problem solving challenge	3 points — Used a large number of original ideas and strategies to solve the game challenge.	2 points — Used several original ideas and strategies to solve the game challenge.	1 point — Rarely used original ideas to solve the game challenges.	0 points — Did not use any original ideas to solve the game challenges.	___/3
Ability to act on constructive feedback	3 points — Readily adapted changes when new and relevant ideas and new information was presented.	2 points — Made changes with some encouragement.	1 point — Hesitated to make changes when new and relevant ideas and information are presented.	0 points — Did not consider new and relevant ideas and information.	___/3
Group/partner teamwork	3 points — All team members contributed equally to the activity's objective.	2 points — Assisted group/partner in the activity's objective.	1 point — Finished individual task, but did not assist group/partner during the activity.	0 points — Contributed little to the group effort during the activity.	___/3
				TOTAL POINTS	___/21

Figure 4-19 Virtual Simulations and Games Rubric (Bell, 2008).

Key Concepts Discussed

1. **Planning Authentic Student Assessment** is a process that includes the following steps: 1) describe the learning context – this involves reviewing and itemizing the course characteristics, the student characteristics, and classroom (virtual -or- face-to-face) characteristics; 2) identifying the stakeholders – an examination of the instructor's goals, the department or institution's objectives, and the needs of the students in order to determine the learning objectives; 3) create the learning objectives – in authentic instruction, these objectives are statements that describe the knowledge, skills, or behaviors students are expected to be able to perform; 4) determine how to use the assessment results – possible uses include informally monitor student work, provide feedback, document progress, or to formally evaluate student knowledge; 5) create an authentic assessment plan – the assessment should include the course learning objectives, the assessment points, the assessment method(s), and the performance criteria for each method.
2. **Types of Rubrics** can be divided into three general categories for performance assessment (Borich, 2008), these being 1) checklists, 2) rating scales, and 3) holistic scoring. Checklist rubrics are used in evaluating student work on performance, and consist of specific pre-established performance criteria. Rating (or analytic) rubrics are the most common and typically include specific point values, and scales. Holistic scoring means there is one overall score instead of discrete dimensions.
3. **Subject Specific Rubrics** are defined by the choice of whether to use a checklist, a holistic, or an analytic approach to scoring. Other factors include the time requirements, the nature of the task itself, and the specific performance criteria being observed (Borich, 2008). Of the many different formats and styles of rubrics, the following is a list of the more commonly used:
    - Comparison/Contrast Essay Rubric
    - Creativity Rubric
    - Data Analysis Rubric
    - Experimental Inquiry Rubric
    - Instrumental Music Rubric
    - Learning Skills Rubric
    - Observation Rubric
    - Oral Presentation Rubric
    - Reflection Paper Rubric
    - Research Paper Rubric
4. **Serious Games and Virtual Simulations** are recreations of real-world events or processes designed for problem solving, training or educating users. Serious games are not a game genre but a category of games with different purposes. Serious games are designed for a large variety of audiences, including primary or secondary education, professionals and consumers. Serious games can be of any genre, use any game technology, and be developed for any platform, but with the common goal of an authentic or performance based assessment of the user (Steinkuehler, et al., 2012; Michael & Chen, 2005; Bell, 2008).

GLOSSARY:
WORDS FOR LITERATE ONLINE TEACHERS

A

Advergames – Games build to promote products or services. Commonly used to increase activity or brand engagement on consumer-facing websites.

Analytic Rubric – An analytic rubric articulates levels of performance for each criterion so the teacher can assess student performance on each criterion.

Ability – Learning outcomes that are complex, multidimensional (knowledge/skills/attitudes), teachable, and transferable to other areas of life (e.g., critical thinking, communication—oral and written, quantitative reasoning, etc.).Analog – A signal that is received in the same form in which it is transmitted, while the amplitude and frequency may vary.

Alternative Assessment – Alternative assessment is any type of assessment in which students create a response to a question. (This is different than assessments in which students choose a response from a list given, such as multiple choice, true/false, or matching). Alternative assessments can include short answer questions, essays, performance assessments, oral presentations, demonstrations, exhibitions, and portfolios.

Amplitude – The amount of variety in a signal. Commonly thought of as the height of a wave. American Standard Code for Information Interexchange (ASCII): A computer language used to convert letters, numbers, and control codes into a digital code understood by most computers.

Anchor Papers – Examples of student performance that serve as a standard against which other papers or performances may be judged are called anchor papers. They are often used as examples of performances at different points on a scoring rubric for a particular grade level. In math problem solving, for example, anchor papers are selected from actual student work that are considered to exemplify the quality of a performance level of "1", "2", "3", and so forth. If used with analytical

Assessment – Assessment is the process of gathering information to make decisions. In an educational context, assessment is the process of observing learning: describing, collecting, recording, scoring, and interpreting information about a student's or one's own learning.

Assessment literacy – Assessment literacy means having knowledge about the basic principles of sound assessment practice, including terminology, the development and use of assessment methodologies and techniques, familiarity with standards of quality in assessment.

Asynchronous gameplay – Players don't have to be online at the same time.

Asynchronous learning – Learning in which interaction between instructors and students occurs intermittently with a time delay. Examples are self-paced courses taken via the Internet or CD-ROM, Q&A mentoring, online discussion groups, and email.

Asynchronous Transmission Mode (ATM) – A method of sending data in irregular time intervals using a code such as ASCII. ATM allows most modern computers to communicate with one another easily.

Audio Bridge – A device used in audioconferencing that connects multiple telephone lines. Audioconferencing: Voice only connection of more than two sites using standard telephone lines.

Augmented Reality Games (ARGs) – Are designed to make it easier to generate the four intrinsic rewards we crave (more satisfying work, better hope for success, stronger social connectivity, and more meaning) whenever we can't or don't want to be in a virtual environment. ARGs are games we play to get more out of our real life, as opposed to games we play to escape it.

Authentic Assessment – Assessments that involve engaging tasks built around important questions/issues reflecting meaningful contexts found in the particular field of study or in adult life. The tasks involved focus on non-routine, multi-stage (i.e., "real") problems, generally requiring students to produce some kind of quality product and/or performance. Authentic assessments are usually accompanied by explicitly-defined standards and criteria shared with students. Note: Some educators choose to distinguish between authentic assessment and performance assessment (see also performance assessment). For these educators, performance assessment meets the above definition except that the tasks do not reflect real-world (authentic) challenges. If we are going to ask students to construct knowledge on assessments, then virtually all such tasks should be authentic in nature or they lose some relevance to the students. Thus, for me, this distinction between performance and authentic assessments becomes insignificant and unnecessary. Consequently, I use authentic assessment and performance assessment synonymously.

Authentic Task – An assignment given to students designed to assess their ability to apply standards-driven knowledge and skills to real-world challenges. A task is considered authentic when 1) students are asked to construct their own responses rather than to select from ones presented; and 2) the task replicates challenges faced in the real world. Good performance on the task should demonstrate, or partly demonstrate, successful completion of one or more standards. The term task is often used synonymously with the term assessment in the field of authentic assessment.

Autotelic – The scientific term using a self-motivated, self-rewarding activity.

Avatar – A virtual representation of a player's character in a game. Common in role-playing games in which the player might take on the role of a magical creature or a medieval warrior.

B

Backbone – A primary communication path connecting multiple users.

Badge – A visual token of an achievement. Usually designed to look like the real-world analogs such as Boy Scout badges or the Good Housekeeping Seal.

Band – A range of frequencies between defined upper and lower limits.

Bandwidth – Information carrying capacity of a communication channel.

Benchmark – A benchmark is point a in time (e.g., 4th grade) that may be used to measure student progress. Benchmarks are designed to help educators organize and make sense of a complex process of interaction between the student, the teacher, and the learning process.

Binary – A computer language developed with only two letters in its alphabet.

Bit – Abbreviation for a single binary digit.

Blog (Web log) – A webpage that serves as a publicly accessible personal journal for an individual. Typically updated daily, blogs often reflect the personality of the author.

Bluetooth – A short-range radio technology aimed at simplifying communications among Internet devices and between devices and the Internet.

Broadband – A type of data transmission in which a single medium (wire) can carry several channels at once. Cable TV, for example, uses broadband transmission. Broadband technology can transmit data, audio, and video all at once over long distances.

Broadcast – To simultaneously send the same message to multiple recipients. Broadcasting is a useful feature in e-mail systems.

Browser – Software that allows you to find and see information on the Internet.

Byte – A single computer word, generally eight bits.

C

C-Learning – Classroom learning. See ILT.

Casual Games – An industry word for games that tend to be easy to learn, quick to play, and require far less computer memory and processing power than other computer and video games. E.g.: Minesweeper, Solitaire, Bejeweled.

CBT – An umbrella term for the use of computers in both instruction and management of the teaching and learning process. CAI (computer-assisted instruction) and CMI (computer-managed instruction) are included under the heading of CBT. Some people use the terms CBT and CAI interchangeably.

Central Processing Unit (CPU) – The component of a computer in which data processing takes place.

Channel – The smallest subdivision of a circuit, usually with a path in only one direction.

Checklists – Checklists are lists of characteristics or behaviors. Checklists are used to guide evaluation of student performances by noting the presence or absence of any given characteristic or behavior.

Classroom-based Assessment/Evidence – An assessment developed, administered, and scored by a teacher or set of teachers with the purpose of evaluating individual or classroom student performance on a topic is known as classroom-based assessment. Ideally, the results of a classroom assessment are used to inform instruction so that students reach high standards. (In Washington State, a classroom-based component is a major part of the state assessment system.)

CMI – Computer Managed Instruction refers to programs that evaluate and diagnose students' needs, guide them though the next step in their learning, and record their progress. Both CMI and CAI (computer programs that provide drill and practice exercises) can be used with little teacher intervention. CEI (computer-enhanced instruction), on the other hand, requires the teacher to be involved in planning and helping to carry out learning activities.

CMS (Course Management System) – Software that automates the administration of a class website. These often include modules for online class discussions, grade books, homework turn-in and pickup, class calendars, and tools to make it easy to upload documents and link to electronic course reserves.

Codec (COder/DECoder) – Device used to convert analog signals to digital signals for transmission and reconvert signals upon reception at the remote site while allowing for the signal to be compressed for less expensive transmission.

Collaboration – A way of working together requiring three distinct kinds of concerted effort: cooperating (acting purposefully toward a common goal), coordinating (synchronizing efforts and sharing resources), and cocreating (producing a novel outcome together).

Competence – The individual's demonstrated capacity to perform, i.e., the possession of knowledge, skills and personal characteristics needed to satisfy the special demands or requirements of a particular situation is referred to as competence.

Compressed Video – When video signals are downsized to allow travel along a smaller carrier.

Compression – Reducing the amount of visual information sent in a signal by only transmitting changes in action.

Computer Assisted Instruction (CAI) – Teaching process in which a computer is utilized to enhance the learning environment by assisting students in gaining mastery over a specific skill.

Content – Information captured digitally and imparted to learners. Formats for e-Learning content include text, audio, video, animation, simulation, and more.

Content Standard – See standard.

Cookie – A message given by a Web server to a Web browser, which stores the message in a text file. The message is then sent back to the server each time the browser requests a page from the server. The main purpose of cookies is to identify users and possibly prepare customized webpages for them. Cookies can be disabled in the browser.

Criteria – Characteristics of good performance on a particular task. For example, criteria for a persuasive essay might include well organized, clearly stated, and sufficient support for arguments.

Cyberspace – The nebulous "place" where humans interact over computer networks. Coined by William Gibson in Neuromancer.

D

Daily/monthly active users (DAUs/MAUs) – The number of individuals who visit your website on an average day or during the course of a month. Common metrics for social games. The ratio of these numbers indicates the intensity of user activity; a DAU/MAU ratio of 50% would mean that half the users visit every day.

Descriptors – Statements of expected performance at each level of performance for a particular criterion in a rubric - typically found in analytic rubrics.

Desktop Videoconferencing – Videoconferencing on a personal computer.

DHTML (Dynamic HTML) – Is the combination of HTML, style sheets and scripts that allows documents to be animated. Dynamic HTML allows a webpage to change after it's loaded into the browser --there doesn't have to be any communication with the Web server for an update.

Dial-Up Teleconference – Using public telephone lines for communications links among various locations.

Digital – An electrical signal that varies in discrete steps in voltage, frequency, amplitude, locations, etc.. Digital signals can be transmitted faster and more accurately than analog signals.

Discussion boards – Forums on the Internet or an intranet where users can post messages for others to read.

Distance education – Educational situation in which the instructor and students are separated by time, location, or both. Education or training courses are delivered to remote locations via synchronous or asynchronous means of instruction, including written correspondence, text, graphics, audio- and videotape, CD-ROM, online learning, audio- and videoconferencing, interactive TV, and FAX. Distance education does not preclude the use of the traditional classroom. The definition of distance education is broader than and entails the definition of e-Learning.

Distance learning – The desired outcome of distance education. The two terms are often used interchangeably.

Distractors – The incorrect alternatives or choices in a selected response item.

Download – Using the network to transfer files from one computer to another.

DVI (Digital Visual Interface) – A digital interface standard created by the Digital Display Working Group (DDWG) to convert analog signals into digital signals to accommodate both analog and digital monitors.

E

Echo Cancellation – The process of eliminating the acoustic echo in a videoconferencing room.

Edutainment – Entertainment media with Educational content. Film, Games, Videogames. Sometimes known as Chocolate covered broccoli.

Electronic Mail (E-mail) – Sending messages from one computer user to another.

E-Learning – E-Learning is the learning process created by interaction with digitally delivered content, services and support. Some categories of E-Learning:

- On-Demand e-Learning – 'jukeboxes' of content available when required.
- Live On-Line e-Learning – multiple learners in multiple sites simultaneously.
- Learning Objects – granular 'chunks' of learning material.
- On-Line Coaching – access to subject matter expertise.
- Knowledge Bases – database access to learning content in a searchable environment.
- Learning Architectures – structures for developing and delivering e-Learning.
- Simulation Based Learning – learning via simulated experience.
- Blended Learning – combining face-to-face classes with technology delivered content.

Encoding – The process of compressing a media file for a specific purpose, such as streaming on the Web. One can encode a file that is in analog form (such as a VHS tape) or one that is already digital (such as the signal on a Mini-DV tape).

Encryption – Encoding information using some specific algorithm in order to hide it. The original information cannot be retrieved without using a matching decryption algorithm.

Essay Test – A test that requires students to answer questions in writing is an essay test. Responses can be brief or extensive. The essay test usually measures knowledge as well as the ability to apply knowledge of a subject to questions about the subject.

Evaluation – Evaluation is the process of making judgments based on criteria and evidence.

Exemplar – Models of excellence are known as exemplars.

Extrinsic motivation – Doing something for a reason other than for its own sake. This could be money, status, power, some other reward you value, direction by your boss, benefits for someone else you care about, etc.

F

Facsimile (FAX) – System used to transmit textual or graphical images over standard telephone lines.

Fiber Optic Cable – Glass fiber that is used for laser transmission of video, audio, and/or data.

File Transfer Protocol (FTP) – A protocol that allows you to move files from a distant computer to a local computer using a network like the Internet.

Firewall – Any of a number of security schemes that prevent unauthorized users from gaining access to a computer network or that monitor transfers of information to and from the network.

File server – A computer on a network with the primary task of storing files that can be shared by network users.

Frequency – The space between waves in a signal. The amount of time between waves passing a stationary point.

Frequently Asked Questions (FAQ) – A collection of information on the basics of any given subject, often used on the WWW.

Full Motion Video – Signal which allows transmission of complete action taking place at the origination site.

Fully Interactive Video – (Two way interactive video) Two sites interact with audio and video as if they were co-located.

G

Game Mechanics – Game mechanics are the mechanisms by which the player achieves the goals of the game. They include the actions that the player can perform like: turn-taking, shooting, collecting, aiming, moving, choosing, and buying.

GB (gigabyte) – Just over one billion bytes. 1,000 megabytes.

GIF (Graphics Interchange Format) – Pronounced jiff or giff (hard g), a file format commonly used for images on the Web. GIFs are especially suitable for images composed of relatively few colors, such as logos or vector graphics.

Goal – In the field of student assessment, a goal is a very broad statement of what students should know or be able to do. Unlike a standard or an objective, a goal is often not written in language that is amenable to assessment. Rather, the purpose for crafting a set of goals typically is to give a brief and broad picture of what a school, district, state, etc. expects its students will know and be able to do upon graduation.

Granularity – The degree of detail something can be broken down into, or the number of discrete components making up any type of system. In e-Learning, granularity is defined by the number of content chunks.

GUI (graphical user interface) – A computer interface using windows, icons, menus and pointers (a WIMP interface), such as Windows.

H

Holistic Rubric – In contrast to an analytic rubric, a holistic rubric does not list separate levels of performance for each criterion. Instead, a holistic rubric assigns a level of performance by assessing performance across multiple criteria as a whole.

Holistic Scoring – In assessment, holistic scoring means assigning a single score based on an overall assessment of performance rather than by scoring or analyzing dimensions individually. The product is considered to be more than the sum of its parts and so the quality of a final product or performance is evaluated. Holistic scoring criteria might combine a number of elements on a single scale.

Home Page – A document with an address (URL) on the World Wide Web maintained by a person or organization which contains pointers to other pieces of information.

Host – A network computer that can receive information from other computers.

HTML (Hypertext Markup Language) – The programming language used to create documents for display on the World Wide Web.

HTTP (Hypertext Transfer Protocol) – The set of rules and standards that govern how information is transmitted on the World Wide Web.

Hypertext – A system for retrieving information from servers on the Internet using World Wide Web client software. Hypertext consists of key words or phrases in a WWW page that are linked electronically to other webpages. The term was coined by pioneering engineer Ted Nelson.

I

ICT – Information and communication technology (ICT). ICT is defined as any computer-based resource, networked or stand alone, hardware or software.

ILS (Integrated Learning System) – A complete software, hardware, and network system used for instruction. In addition to providing curriculum and lessons organized by level, an ILS usually includes a number of tools such as assessments, record keeping, report writing, and user information files that help to identify learning needs, monitor progress, and maintain student records.

ILT (instructor-led training) – Usually refers to traditional classroom training, in which an instructor teaches a course to a room of learner s. The term is used synonymously with on-site training and classroom training (C-Learning).

IMS (Instructional Management System) – Global Learning Consortium. IMS is a global coalition of academic, commercial and government organizations, working together to define the Internet architecture for learning. IMS is focusing on developing technical specifications that will support a broad range of learning with a global perspective. Their specification development supports the needs of K-12, higher education and training around the world.

Interoperability – The ability of hardware or software components to work together effectively.

IP (Internet Protocol) – IP is the basic language of the Internet. It was developed by the government for use in connecting multiple computer networks.

IP address – Abbreviation for Internet Protocol Address, the addressing system used in the Internet, assigning all connected devices a unique identification number.

ISDN (Integrated Services Digital Network) – A telecommunications standard allowing communications channels to carry voice, video, and data simultaneously.

ISO (International Organization for Standardization) – An international federation of national standards bodies.

IT (Information Technology) – The industry or discipline involving the collection, dissemination, and management of data, typically through the use of computers.

ITFS (Instructional Television Fixed Service) – Microwave-based, high-frequency television used in educational program delivery.

J

Java – An object-oriented programming language developed by Sun Microsystems. Java isn't dependent on specific hardware and can be launched from within an HTML document or stand-alone.

Java applet – A small Java program that usually executes within a Web browser.

JISC – The Joint Information Systems Committee is an independent advisory body that supports further and higher education by providing strategic guidance, advice and opportunities to use Information and Communications Technology (ICT) to support teaching, learning, research and administration.

JPEG (Joint Photographic Experts Group) – Refers to an image file format popular for delivery over the Web because of its relatively high quality and low file size. Before uploading JPEGs to the Web, users can determine the amount of compression assigned to them-usually on a scale from 1 to 10. Recommended file type for photographic images.

Just-in-time (JIT) – Characteristic of e-Learning in which learners are able to access the information they need exactly when they need it.

K

Knowledge management – The process of capturing, organizing, and storing information and experiences of workers and groups within an organization and making it available to others. By collecting those artifacts in a central or distributed electronic environment (often in a database called a knowledge base), KM aims to help a company gain competitive advantage.

L

LAN (Local Area Network) – Two or more local computers that are physically connected.

LCMS (Learning Content Management System) – An LCMS provides an authoring application, a data repository, a delivery interface, and administration tools. The authoring tools provide templates and storyboarding capabilities, and may be used to convert existing content. Some LCMS's offer collaboration tools, including chat, integrated email, and threaded discussion groups.

Learning environment – The physical or virtual setting in which learning takes place.

Learning object – A reusable, media-independent collection of information used as a modular building block for e-Learning content. Learning objects are most effective when organized by a meta data classification system and stored in a data repository such as an LCMS.

Learning platforms – Internal or external sites often organized around tightly focused topics, which contain technologies (ranging from chat rooms to groupware) that enable users to submit and retrieve information.

Learning portal – Any website that offers learners or organizations consolidated access to learning and training resources from multiple sources. Operators of learning portals are also called content aggregators, distributors, or hosts.

Listserv – An e-mail program that allows multiple computer users to connect onto a single system, creating an online discussion.

Learning solution – (1) Any combination of technology and methodology that delivers learning. (2) Software and/or hardware products that suppliers tout as answers to business training needs. This territory is a recent annexation to the business landscape.

Link (aka hyperlink) – The result of HTML markup signifying to a browser that data within a document will automatically connect with either nested data or an outside source. Used in the design of hypertext.

LISTSERV – E-mail list management software developed by L-Soft International.

LMS (learning management system) – Software that automates the administration of training. The LMS registers users, tracks courses in a catalog, records data from learners; and provides reports to management. An LMS is typically designed to handle courses by multiple publishers and providers. It usually doesn't include its own authoring capabilities; instead, it focuses on managing courses created by a variety of other sources.

Localization – The tailoring of an offering to meet the specific needs of a geographic area, product, or target audience.

M

Meta data – Information about content that enables it to be stored in and retrieved from a database.

Metatag – An HTML tag identifying the contents of a website. Information commonly found in the metatag includes copyright info, key words for search engines, and formatting descriptions of the page.

Microworld – A Microworld is a term coined at the MIT Media Lab Learning and Common Sense Group . It means, literally, a tiny world inside which a student can explore alternatives, test hypotheses, and discover facts that are true about that world. It differs from a simulation in that the student is encouraged to think about it as a "real" world, and not simply as a simulation of another world

MLE (Managed Learning Environment) – The term MLE refers to the whole rang e of information systems and processes of a college or university (including its VLE if it has one) that contribute directly, or indirectly, to learning and the management of that learning. There is sometimes confusion between a VLE and a MLE. The term Virtual Learning Environment (VLE) is one possible component of a MLE: it refers to the component(s) within an MLE that provides the "online" interactions of various kinds which can take place between learners and tutors, including online learning.

M-learning – Mobile learning. This is facilitated via a wireless device such as a PDA, a smart phone or a laptop.

MPEG (Moving Picture Experts Group) – A series of International Organization for Standardization (ISO) standards for digital video and audio, designed for different uses and data rates.

- MPEG-1: a standard designed to allow for playback of video on CD. VCDs are encoded with MPEG-1. This format has dimensions of 352x240 pixels, and is sometimes considered comparable to VHS in quality. The bit rate of a standard MPEG1 is 1.5Mbps. Included in MPEG-1 is a popular standard for audio called MP3 (MP3 is technically MPEG-1 layer 3)

- MPEG-2: the standard for DVD video. Supports higher data rates than MPEG-1.
- MPEG-7: an emerging standard for describing multimedia objects so that they can be accessed in a database. MPEG-7 will allow users to access video based on elements such as instances of a particular color or shape

Multicasting – The transmission of information to more than one recipient. For example, sending an e-mail message to a list of people. Teleconferencing and videoconferencing can also use multicasting.

Multimedia – Any document which uses multiple forms of communication, such as text, audio, and/or video.

Multi-Point Control Unit (MCU) – Computerized switching system which allows point-to-multipoint videoconferencing.

N

Navigation – Finding your way from page to page on the World Wide Web.

Netiquette – Online manners; the rules of conduct for online or Internet users.

Netscape Navigator – Browser software that enables users to view webpages.

Network – Two or more computers that are connected so users can share files and devices (for example, printers, servers, and storage devices).

NTSC (National Television System Committee) – The video input signal formats used in North America and Japan. Full-sized NTSC has a display rate of 60 fields per second (30 interlaced fps), and 525 total lines (480 visible) per frame.

O

Objective – Much like a goal or standard, an objective is a statement of what students should know and be able to do. Typically, an objective is the most narrow of these statements, usually describing what a student should know or be able to do at the end of a specific lesson plan. Like a standard, an objective is amenable to assessment, that is, it is observable and measurable.

Online community – A meeting place for people on the Internet. Designed to facilitate interaction and collaboration among people who share common interests and needs. Online communities can be open to all or by membership only and may or may not offer moderator tools.

Online – Active and prepared for operation. Also suggests access to a computer network.

Operant conditioning – A theory and process developed by psychologist B. F. Skinner in which behaviors are modified by rewards (and, in some approaches, by punishment also).

Origination Site – The location from which a teleconference originates.

Outcome – An operationally defined educational goal, usually a culminating activity, product or performance that can be measured is referred to as an outcome.

P

Packet – A bundle of data transmitted over a network. Packets have no set size; they can range from one character to hundreds of characters.

PDA (Personal Digital Assistant) – Handheld computer device used to organize personal information such as contacts, schedules, and so forth. Data can usually be transferred to a desktop computer by cable or wireless transmission.

PDF (Portable Document Format) – File format developed by Adobe Systems to enable users of any hardware or software platform to view documents exactly as they were created — with fonts, images, links, and layouts as they were originally designed.

Peer-to-peer network (P2P) – A communication network that enables users to connect their computers and share files directly with other users without having to go through a centralized server. Groove is an example of an application that runs on a peer-to-peer network.

Performance-based Assessment – Performance-based assessment refers to systematic observation and rating of student performance of an educational objective. Such assessment is often an ongoing observation over a period of time, and typically requires the student to finish products. The assessment may be a continuing interaction between teacher and student and should ideally be part of the learning process. The assessment should be a real-world performance with relevance to the student and learning community. Assessment of the performance is done using a scoring guide or rubric.

Performance Criteria – A description of the characteristics that will be considered when a performance task is judged are called performance criteria. Performance criteria are often defined in a rubric or scoring guide are referred to as holistic, or analytical trait; general, or specific. Anchor papers or benchmark performances may be used to identify each level of competency in the rubric or scoring guide.

Performance Standards – Performance standards provide clear statements of the kinds of performances that constitute evidence that students had met the content standards. They answer the question, how well must a student perform? For example, we can set up assessments that correspond to our curriculum standards (say, mathematical problem solving), and then specify the level and kind of responses students need to give in order to be considered skilled (performance standards). (Also see Benchmark and Anchor Performances).

Performance Task – A performance task gives the student the opportunity to illustrate, perform, or demonstrate what they know and can do.

Pixel (picture element) – Tiny dots that make up a computer image. The more pixels a computer monitor can display, the better the image resolution and quality. On a color monitor, every pixel is composed of a red, a green, and a blue dot that are small enough to appear as a single entity.

Play – An essentially unconstrained experience if spontaneous fun, contrasted with the structured rules-based systems of games.

Play testing – Trying out a game with actual players as a way of garnering feedback.

Plug-in – An accessory program that adds capabilities to the main program. Used on webpages to display multimedia content.

PNG (Portable Network Graphics) – The patent-free graphics compression format developed by Macromedia expected to replace GIF. PNG offers advanced graphics features such as 48-bit color.

Point-to-Point – Transmission between two locations.

Point-to-Multipoint – Transmission between multiple locations using a bridge.

POP (Point of Presence) – Point of connection between an interexchange carrier and a local carrier to pass communications into the network.

Portfolio – A purposeful collection of student work that tells the story or his/her growth as a learner is called a portfolio. There are many kinds of portfolios. The usefulness (for assessment and instruction) of any portfolio is enhanced by performance criteria, student involvement, and student self-reflection.

Portfolio Assessment – Portfolios may be assessed in a variety of ways. Each piece may be individually scored, or the portfolio might be assessed merely for the presence of required pieces, or a holistic scoring process might be used and an evaluation made on the basis of an overall impression of the student's collected work. It is common that assessors work together to establish consensus of standards or to ensure greater reliability in evaluation of student work. Established criteria are often used by reviewers and students involved in the process of evaluating progress and achievement of objectives.

PPP – A software package which allows a user to have a direct connection to the Internet over a telephone line.

Process Standards – Statements that describe skills students should develop to enhance the process of learning. Process standards are not specific to a particular discipline, but are generic skills that are applicable to any discipline (e.g., students will find and evaluate relevant information).

Protocol – A formal set of standards, rules, or formats for exchanging data that assures uniformity between computers and applications.

Pull technology – In reference to the Internet or other online services, the technology whereby people use software such as a Web browser to locate and "pull down" information for themselves.

Push technology – In reference to the Internet or other online services, the technology whereby information is sent directly to a user's computer.

Q

Quest – A specific mission or challenge for players of a game. The quest will usually have a narrative and an objective and a reward for completion.

QuickTime – A digital audio and video file-format and architecture developed by Apple Computer, Inc. Can be viewed on most computing platforms.

QuickTime VR (QTVR) – A part of the QuickTime architecture that allows 360-degree interactive panoramas to be developed and viewed. (VR = virtual reality)

R

RAM (Random Access Memory) – Temporary storage built into a computer system that functions as a "workspace" for data and program instructions.

Rating Scales – A scale based on descriptive words or phrases that indicate performance levels is called a rating scale. Qualities of a performance are described (e.g., advanced, intermediate, novice) in order to designate a level of achievement. The scale may be used with rubrics or descriptions of each level of performance.

RealMedia – One of the first CODECs for delivering streaming video over the Internet. Like other CODECs, RealMedia (comprised of RealVideo, RealAudio, and other file formats created by Real) use compression algorithms for eliminating data that can be considered as extraneous or not as important as other information. RealMedia and Windows Media are the two most widely used technologies for streaming video today.

Real-time communication – Communication in which information is received at (or nearly at) the instant it's sent. Real-time communication is a characteristic of synchronous learning.

Reliability – Reliability is the measure of consistency for an assessment instrument. The instrument should yield similar results over time with similar populations in similar circumstances.

Rubric – A rubric is an established set of criteria for scoring or rating students' performance on tests, portfolios, writing samples, or other performance tasks.

Resolution – The number of pixels in a given space, usually measured as dots per inch (DPI). Also, the number of dots per inch used by an output device.

Reusable – E-Learning content that can be transferred to various infrastructures or delivery mechanisms, usually without changes.

RIO (reusable information object) – A collection of content, practice, and assessment items assembled around a single learning objective. RIOs are built from templates based on whether the goal is to communicate a concept, fact, process, principle, or procedure. (Pronounced "REE-O")

RLO (reusable learning object) – A collection of RIOs, overview, summary, and assessments that supp orts a specific learning objective.

S

Scalability – The degree to which a computer application or component can be expanded in size, volume, or number of users served and continue to function properly.

Scanner – A device that converts a printed page or image into an digital representation that can be viewed and manipulated on a computer.

Scoring Criteria – Scoring criteria are rules for assigning a score or rating a student's performance on tests, portfolios, writing samples, or other performance tasks. Scoring criteria may include rating scales, checklists, answer keys, and other scoring tools.

Scoring Guide – A package of guidelines intended for people scoring performance assessments. May include instructions or raters, notes on training raters, rating scales, samples of student work exemplifying various levels of performance.

SCORM (Sharable Content Object Reference Model) – SCORM is a set of interrelated technical specifications built upon the work of the AICC, IMS and IEEE to create one unified content model. These specifications enable the reuse of Web-based learning content across multiple environments. SCORM dictates how an LMS must make the API (Application Program Interface) available to the content, so content developers know exactly how to write the JavaScript code to locate and call the API.

Section 508 – The section of the 1998 Rehabilitation Act that states that all electronic and information technology procured, used, or developed by the federal government after June 25, 2001, must be accessible to people with disabilities. Affected technology includes hardware such as copiers, fax machines, telephones, and other electronic devices as well as application software and Web sites. See http://www.section508.gov/.

Self-Determination Theory – A psychological theory developed by Edwards Deci and Richard Ryan of the University of Rochester along with many collaborators, which defines and emphasizes the importance of intrinsic motivation.

Selected Response Items – Selected response items are those that give the student choice and the student must select a response. These include multiple-choice, true-false, and matching items.

Self-Assessment – Self-assessment is the process of doing a systematic review of one's own performance, usually for the purpose of improving future performance. Such assessment may involve comparison with a standard, established criteria. Self-assessment may involve critiquing one's own work or may be a simple description of one's performance.

Semantic Web, The – The Semantic Web provides a common framework that allows data to be shared and reused across application, enterprise, and community boundaries. It is a collaborative effort led by W3C with participation from a large number of researchers and industrial partners. It is based on the Resource Description Framework (RDF), which integrates a variety of applications using XML for syntax and URIs for naming. A concept proposed by World Wide Web inventor Tim Berners-Lee.

Serious games – Games created for a purpose other than enjoyment; typically some form of knowledge or skill development.

Server – A computer with a special service function on a network, generally receiving and connecting incoming information traffic.

Simulations – Highly interactive applications that allow the learner to model or role-play in a scenario. Simulations enable the learner to practice skills or behaviors in a risk-free environment.

Social games – Online games delivered through social networks, primarily Facebook, often with a significant element of social interaction. The most successful social games developer is Zynga, publisher of FarmVille, Words with Friends, Mafia Wars and Draw Something.

Social graph – The network of relationships among friends such as the matrix of connections on Facebook or other social networking sites.

Source code – Program instructions written by a software developer and later translated(usually by a compiler) into machine language that a computer can understand.

Spam - (noun) Junk e-mail that is sent, unsolicited and in bulk, to advertise products or services or publicize a message. The term may have originated from a Monty Python skit; (verb) To send unsolicited bulk e-mail to advertise products or services or publicize a message.

SMIL (Synchronized Multimedia Integration Language) – A markup language based on XML that allows you to create and stream Web-based presentations composed of multiple media types, such as images, text, video, and audio.

Standard – A description of the outcomes or expectations of achievement which serves as a basis for defining more specific performance criteria and making assessment judgments (sometimes referred to as content standards as opposed to performance standards). (Note: while meeting a specific standard may be selected as a goal, not all goal statements are written specifically enough to be used as a standard).

Standardized Test – A test that is given and scored in a uniform manner is known as a standardized test. These tests are carefully constructed and items are selected after trials for appropriateness and difficulty. Tests are issued with a manual giving complete guidelines for administration and scoring. The guidelines attempt to eliminate extraneous interference that might influence test results. Standardized tests may produce norm-referenced or criterion-referenced information.

Stem – A question or statement followed by a number of choices or alternatives that answer or complete the question or statement.

Streaming media (streaming audio or video) – Audio or video files played as they are being downloaded over the Internet instead of user s having to wait for the entire file to download first. Requires a media player, such as RealPlayer, QuickTime Player or Windows Media Player.

Synchronous learning – A real-time, instructor-led online learning event in which all participants are logged on at the same time and communicate directly with each other. In this virtual classroom setting, the instructor maintains control of the class, with the ability to "call on" participants. In most platforms, students and teachers can use a whiteboard to see work in progress and share knowledge. Interaction may also occur via audio- or videoconferencing, Internet telephony, or two-way live broadcasts.

T

T-1 (DS-1) – High speed digital data channel that is a high volume carrier of voice and/or data. Often used for compressed video teleconferencing. T-1 has 24 voice channels.

T-3 (DS-3) – A digital channel which communicates at a significantly faster rate than T-1.

Task – A task is anything from a discrete multiple-choice or short-answer item to a complex project requiring students to use many different types of learning to solve a problem, investigate a situation, write a story, or do any other real-world task. The task is a whole. Within a task there may be several dependent items.

TCP (Transmission Control Protocol) – A protocol which makes sure that packets of data are shipped and received in the intended order.

Telecommunication – The science of information transport using wire, radio, optical, or electromagnetic channels to transmit receive signals for voice or data communications using electrical means.

Teleconferencing – Two way electronic communication between two or more groups in separate locations via audio, video, and/or computer systems.

Telnet – The Internet protocol in the TCP/IP suite that enables a user to interact with a program that is running in another computer; the name of the program used for remote login.

Thinking Skills – Thinking skills include thinking analytically, logically and creatively to form reasoned judgments and solve problems.

TIFF (Tagged Image File Format) – A widely supported file format for storing bit-mapped images on personal computers. TIFF graphics can be any resolution, black and white, gray-scaled, or color. Files in TIFF format usually end with a .tif extension. TIFF files are often used for archiving high quality versions of an image, such as images intended to be reproduced in print or studied digitally in minute detail.

Thin client – (1) A network computer without disk drives that accesses programs and data from a server instead of storing them locally. (2) Software that performs the majority of its operations on a server rather than the local computer, thus requiring less memory and fewer plug-ins.

Transponder – Satellite transmitter and receiver that receives and amplifies a signal prior to re-transmission to an earth station.

Trojan horse – A malicious computer program that appears legitimate but masks a destructive file or application. Unlike viruses, Trojan horses usually do not replicate themselves but can still cause a great deal of damage, such as creating an entryway into your computer for malevolent users.

U

UNIX – A popular multi-user, multitasking operating system developed at Bell Labs in the early 1970s. Created by just a handful of programmers, UNIX was designed to be a small, flexible system used exclusively by programmers. UNIX was one of the first operating systems to be written in a high-level programming language, namely C. This meant that it could be installed on virtually any computer for which a C compiler existed. This natural portability combined with its low price made it a popular choice among universities.

Uplink – The communication link from the transmitting earth station to the satellite.

Upload – To copy data from your computer to another computer over a computer network, the opposite of download.

URI (uniform resource identifier) – The name and address of information (text, graphics, audio, video etc.) on the Internet. A URI usually identifies the application used to access the resource, the machine the resource is located on, and the file name of the resource. A webpage address or URL is the most commonly used type of URI.

URL (uniform resource locator) – The address of a page on the World Wide Web. e.g. http://www.tbuck.us

V

V-Learning – Learning that takes place in a Virtual Environment, or Multi User Virtual Environment (MUVE).

Value Standards – Statements that describe attitudes teachers would like students to develop towards learning (e.g., students will value diversity of opinions or perspectives).

Validity – Validity refers to the extent to which the assessment measures the desired performance and appropriate inferences can be drawn from the results. A valid assessment accurately reflects the learning it was designed to measure.

Variable reward schedule – A prize or reward delivered on some non-predictable basis, such as the pay off of a slot machine. Contrasted with fixed interval rewards (guaranteed at regular time periods) or fixed-ratio rewards (guaranteed for a certain amount of activity).

Video Teleconferencing – A teleconference including two way video.

Virtual classroom – The online learning space where students and instructors interact

Virtual community – See online community.

Virtual reality (VR) – An artificial computer-generated environment that is experienced through sensory stimuli and in which special equipment allows the user to interact with the simulation.

Virtual world – A persistent online community that allows for virtual interaction between players. Typically worlds involve immersive 3D environments, although it is not essential. Most are online role-playing games, but virtual worlds, such as Second Life, have no gameplay objectives.

Virus – A destructive type of computer program that attempts to disrupt the normal operation of a computer, rewrite or delete information from storage devices, and in some cases, cause physical damage to the computer.

Virus detection program – A software program to detect, diagnose, and destroy computer viruses

VLE – See MLE

VPN (Virtual Private Network) – A private network configured inside a public network. Offers the security of private networks with the economies of scale and built-in management capabilities of public networks.

VRML (Virtual Reality Modeling Language) – Pronounced ver-mal, VRML is a specification for displaying 3-dimensional objects on the World Wide Web. You can think of it as the 3-D equivalent of HTML. Files written in VRML have a .wrl extension (short for world). To view these files, you need a VRML browser or a VRML plug-in to a Web browser.

W

W3C (World Wide Web Consortium) – An organization developing interoperable specifications, software, and tools for the WWW. See the W3C website at http://www.w3.org/.

WAP (Wireless Application Protocol) – Specification that allows Internet content to be read by wireless devices.

WBT (Web Based Training) – Delivery of educational content via a Web browser over the public Internet, a private intranet, or an extranet. Web-based training often provides links to other learning resources such as references, email, bulletin boards, and discussion groups. WBT also may include a facilitator who can provide course guidelines, manage discussion boards, deliver lectures, and so forth. When used with a facilitator, WBT offers some advantages of instructor-led training while also retaining the advantages of computer-based training.

WCS (Web Communications Services) – MIT Information Services and Technology's Web Communications Services group.

Win state – The outcomes of a game that constitute "winning". Typically defined by the rules of the games and the game's feedback or rewards mechanisms.

WWW (World *Wide Web)* – A graphical hypertext-based Internet tool that provides access to homepages created by individuals, businesses, and other organizations.

X

XHTML (eXtensible Hypertext Markup Language) – Is a reformulation of HTML as an application of XML. It provides the bridge for Web designers to enter the Web of the future, while still being able to maintain compatibility with today's HTML 4 browsers.

XML (Extensible Markup Language) – The next-generation webpage coding language that allows site designers to program their own markup commands, which can then be used as if they were standard HTML commands.

XSL (eXtensible Stylesheet Language or eXtensible Style Language) – A webpage design language that creates style sheets for XML pages, which separate style from content so that developers can specify how and where information is displayed on the page.

Z

Zip – A popular data compression format. Files that have been compressed with the Zip format are called Zip files and usually end with a .ZIP extension.

Zip disk – Portable storage disk that can hold 100 or 250 MB of information, manufactured by the Iomega corporation. Used in a Zip drive, Zip disks can archive or back up large amounts of data.

Zip drive – A high-capacity floppy disk drive developed by Iomega Corporation. Zip disks are slightly larger than conventional floppy disks, and about twice as thick. They can hold 100 or 250 MB of data. Because they're relatively inexpensive and durable, they have become a popular medium for backing up hard disks and for transporting large files.

Zip file – (1) A file that has been compressed, often with the .ZIP format originated by PKWARE. (2) A file on a Zip disk, not necessarily compressed. (3) A compressed file with the .EXE extension that is self-extracting (can be unzipped simply by opening it).

ANNOTATED BIBLIOGRAPHY

Andrade, H. G. 2000. *Using rubrics to promote thinking and learning.* Educational Leadership 57 (5): 13–18.

<u>Abstract</u>: Instructional rubrics, concerned with gradations of quality, are easy to use and explain, communicate teacher expectations clearly, provide students with constructive feedback, and support learning, skill development, understanding, and good thinking. Tips for constructing rubrics and encouraging student participation and self-evaluation are provided.

Anderson, L.W., & Krathwohl (Eds.). (2010). *A Taxonomy for Learning, Teaching, and Assessing: A Revision of Bloom's Taxonomy of Educational Objectives.* New York: Longman.

<u>Abstract</u>: Merl Wittrock, a cognitive psychologist who had proposed a generative model of learning, was an essential member of the group that over a period of 5 years revised the "Taxonomy of Educational Objectives," originally published in 1956. This article describes the development of that 2001 revision (Anderson and Krathwohl, Editors) and Merl's contributions to that effort.

Arbaugh, J. B., Cleveland-Innes, M., Diaz, S. R., Garrison, D. R., Ice, P., Richardson, J. C., et al. (2008). Developing a community of inquiry instrument: Testing a measure of the Community of Inquiry framework using a multi-institutional sample. *The Internet and Higher Education,* 11(3-4), 133-136.

<u>Abstract</u>: This article reports on the multi-institutional development and validation of an instrument that attempts to operationalize Garrison, Anderson and Archer's Community of Inquiry (CoI) framework (2000). The results of the study suggest that the instrument is a valid, reliable, and efficient measure of the dimensions of social presence and cognitive presence, thereby providing additional support for the validity of the CoI as a framework for constructing effective online learning environments. While factor analysis supported the idea of teaching presence as a construct, it also suggested that the construct consisted of two factors--one related to course design and organization and the other related to instructor behavior during the course. The article concludes with a discussion of potential implications of further refinement of the CoI measures for researchers, designers, administrators, and instructors.

Asmus, E. P. (2002). *Instrumental Music Rubric.* January 2002 Florida Music Educators Association In-Service Meeting in Tampa, Florida

> Author's Description: This rubric was developed as part of a session on ensemble assessment held at the January 2002 Florida Music Educators Association In-Service Meeting in Tampa, Florida. The rubric was developed as part of a group activity that was focused on producing a rubric that met the achievement standard levels of the National Music Standards established by the National Association for Music Education (MENC).

Authentic Education. (2011). *What is Understanding by Design?* Retrieved from http://www.authenticeducation.org/ubd/ubd.lasso

> Author's Description: Developed by nationally recognized educators Grant Wiggins and Jay McTighe, and published by the Association for Supervision and Curriculum Development (ASCD), Understanding by Design is based on the following key ideas:
> - A primary goal of education should be the development and deepening of student understanding.
> - Students reveal their understanding most effectively when they are provided with complex, authentic opportunities to explain, interpret, apply, shift perspective, empathize, and self-assess. When applied to complex tasks, these "six facets" provide a conceptual lens through which teachers can better assess student understanding.
> - Effective curriculum development reflects a three-stage design process called "backward design" that delays the planning of classroom activities until goals have been clarified and assessments designed. This process helps to avoid the twin problems of "textbook coverage" and "activity-oriented" teaching, in which no clear priorities and purposes are apparent.
> - Student and school performance gains are achieved through regular reviews of results (achievement data and student work) followed by targeted adjustments to curriculum and instruction. Teachers become most effective when they seek feedback from students and their peers and use that feedback to adjust approaches to design and teaching.
> - Teachers, schools, and districts benefit by "working smarter" through the collaborative design, sharing, and peer review of units of study.

Bangert, A. W. (2009). Building a validity argument for the community of inquiry survey instrument. *Internet and Higher Education, 12(2),* 104-111.

> Abstract: The purpose of this study was to provide empirical evidence to support the validity of the Community of Inquiry (CoI) model survey. The participants for this study were undergraduate and graduate students (n = 1173) enrolled in fully online (57%) and blended online courses (43%) offered through WebCT during the spring 2008 semester at a mid-sized

western university. One half of the student responses were randomly selected for exploratory factor analysis while the remaining half was subjected to confirmatory factor analysis. Results from the exploratory analysis identified a three factor model which was tested through confirmatory factor analysis and found to be an acceptable fit to the predicted population model. Results from this study suggest that the CoI survey holds promise as a useful evaluation tool for providing formative and summative feedback about the effectiveness of online courses and programs.

Bailey, K. M. (1998). Learning about language assessment: dilemmas, decisions, and directions. US: Heinle & Heinle.

Book Description: Learning About Language Assessment is one volume of the authoritative 13-title Teacher Source Series. The author examines the issue of classroom assessment form three distinct perspectives: Teachers' Voices, which are authentic accounts of teachers' experiences; Frameworks, which are comprehensive discussions of theoretical issues; and Investigations, which are inquiry-based activities.

Bennett, R. E. (1997). Reinventing assessment: Speculations on the future of large-scale educational testing. ETS *(Educational Testing Service)*. Policy Information Center: Princeton, NJ.

Abstract: This Policy Information Perspective presents a scenario for the future of testing that divides into three generations of assessment distinguished by the purpose of testing, test format and content, test delivery location, and use of new technology.

Bell, A. (2008). *Serious Games Rubric*. University of Wisconsin-Stout. Retrieved from: http://www.uwstout.edu/soe/profdev/rubrics.cfm

Authors' Description: A collection of rubrics for assessing portfolios, cooperative learning, research process/ report, PowerPoint, podcast, oral presentation, webpage, blog, wiki, and other Web 2.0 projects.

Bente, G. & Breuer, J. (2009). *Making the implicit explicit: embedded measurement in serious games*, in Serious Games: Mechanisms and Effects, U. Ritterfield, M. J. Cody, and P. Vorderer, Eds., pp. 322–343, Routledge, New York, NY, USA, 2009.

Book Description: Serious Games provides a thorough exploration of the claim that playing games can provide learning that is deep, sustained and transferable to the real world. "Serious games" is defined herein as any form of interactive computer-based game software for one or multiple players to be used on any platform and that has been developed to provide more than entertainment to players. With this volume, the editors address the gap in existing scholarship on gaming, providing an academic overview on the mechanisms and effects of serious games. Contributors investigate the psychological mechanisms that take place not only during gaming, but also in game selection, persistent play, and gaming impact.

The work in this collection focuses on the desirable outcomes of digital game play. The editors distinguish between three possible effects -- learning, development, and change -- covering a broad range of serious games' potential impact. Contributions from internationally recognized scholars focus on five objectives:
- Define the area of serious games
- Elaborate on the underlying theories that explain suggested psychological mechanisms elicited through serious game play, addressing cognitive, affective and social processes
- Summarize the empirical evidence on the effectiveness of serious games,
- Introduce innovative research methods as a response to methodological challenges imposed through interactive media
- Discuss the possibilities and limitations of selected applications for educational purposes.

Anchored primarily in social science research, the reader will be introduced to approaches that focus on the gaming process and the users' experiences. Additional perspectives will be provided in the concluding chapters, written from non-social science approaches by experts in academic game design and representatives of the gaming industry. The editors acknowledge the necessity for a broader interdisciplinary study of the phenomena and work to overcome the methodological divide in games research to look ahead to a more integrated and interdisciplinary study of digital games.

Binsubaih, A., Maddock, S., & Romano, D. (2006). A Serious Game for Traffic Accident Investigators. *Interactive Technology and Smart Education, v3*(4), 329-346.

Abstract: In Dubai, traffic accidents kill one person every 37 hours and injure one person every 3 hours. Novice traffic accident investigators in the Dubai police force are expected to "learn by doing" in this intense environment. Currently, they use no alternative to the real world in order to practice. This paper argues for the use of an alternative learning environment, where the novice investigator can feel safe in exploring different investigative routes without fear for the consequences. The paper describes a game-based learning environment that has been built using a game engine. The effectiveness of this environment in improving the performance of traffic accident investigators is also presented. Fifty-six policemen took part in an experiment involving a virtual traffic accident scenario. They were divided into two groups: novices (0 to 2 years experience) and experienced personnel (with more than 2 years experience). The experiment revealed significant performance improvements in both groups, with the improvement reported in novices significantly higher than the one reported in experienced personnel. Both groups showed significant differences in navigational patterns (e.g. distances travelled and time utilization) between the two training sessions.

Boyd-Batstone, P. (2006). *Focused Anecdotal Records Assessment (ARA): a standards based tool for authentic assessment.* In (Shelby Barrentine & Sandra Stokes, Editors) Reading Assessment: Principles and practices for elementary teachers. Newark, DE: International Reading Association Publications.

Book Description: How do you respond to the competing pressures of school accountability, high-stakes testing, classroom assessment and instruction? This updated collection of articles from The Reading Teacher can help. You'll find tools for building school assessment policies, helping students succeed on high-stakes tests, using assessment to inform your instruction, drawing students into the assessment process, and choosing assessment protocols for individual students or groups of students. A list of articles for further reading and IRA's position statement on high-stakes testing will further broaden your knowledge base of assessment issues.

Boyd-Batstone, P. (2006). *Differentiated Early Literacy for English Language Learners: Practical Strategies.* Boston, MA: Allyn & Bacon.

Book Description: The author draws on a wealth of classroom experience working with teachers and students to create a book that gives readers the critical information they need to teach English language learners in an accessible format. This book is packed with strategies and activities that are directly applicable to the classroom and that focus on meeting the early literacy demands of No Child Left Behind. Early literacy strategies for English language learners are differentiated according five levels of language proficiency. The book includes a wealth of tips for parent involvement, offering ways parents, who may not be literate in English, can help their child develop literacy skills. Assessment tools for differentiating levels of English proficiency are included throughout to help pre-service and in-service teachers assess levels of English proficiency in order to differentiate instruction.

Boyd-Batstone, P., Larson, L., & Cox, C. (2004). Teaching and Learning in a Virtual World: A on-line video case studies model based on a language arts methods textbook for pre-service teachers. National Forum of Teacher Education Journal, (November publication date).

Authors' Description: What are the realities and possibilities of utilizing on-line virtual worlds as teaching tools for specific literary works? Through engaging and surprising stories from classrooms where virtual worlds are in use, this book invites readers to understand and participate in this emerging and valuable pedagogy. It examines the experience of high school and college literature teachers involved in a pioneering project to develop virtual worlds for literary study, detailing how they created, utilized, and researched different immersive and interactive virtual reality environments to support the teaching of a wide range of literary works. Readers see how students role-play as literary characters, extending and altering character conduct in purposeful ways ,and how they explore on-line, interactive literature maps, museums, archives, and game worlds to analyze the impact of historical and cultural setting, language, and dialogue on literary characters and events. This book breaks exciting ground, offering insights, pedagogical suggestions, and ways for readers to consider the future of this innovative approach to teaching literary texts.

Boyd-Batstone, P. (2004). Focused Anecdotal Records Assessment (ARA): a standards based tool for authentic assessment. *Reading Teacher,* v58 n3, 230-239.

Abstract: This article describes the tension between standards-based assessment on a macro level and authentic assessment on a micro level. Content standards arguably supply systematic criteria for quantitative measures to report trends and establish policy. Qualitative measures, such as rubrics, student profiles, and observational records, fill in the gaps to give teachers immediate feedback for instructional planning. The purpose of the article is to describe an observational tool for standards-based authentic assessment. Focused anecdotal records assessment (ARA) is a collection of techniques for recording, maintaining, and analyzing observational records. Five components are described: (1) observing children in instructional settings, (2) maintaining a standards-based focus, (3) recording anecdotal records, (4) managing anecdotal records, and (5) using anecdotal records for assessment. The article includes formats for recording specific standards, observational data, summaries of strengths and needs, and instructional recommendations. Focused ARAs help organize assessment data and facilitate communication with students, parents, and other members of the educational community.

Buck, T. L. (2011). Technology literacy recommendations: A review of common college and university entry level standards. *Journal of Research on Technology in Education,* v43, n4, 235-239.

Abstract: This document provides information about common college and university entry level standards recommended by twenty-five regional colleges and universities, and include evaluations of or guides to adult courseware literacy.

Buck, T. L. (2010). *Dr. Buck's AP Computer Science curriculum map*. Retrieved from: http://www.rubrics4assessment.net/curriculum.htm

Author's Description: This is a curriculum map that I created for an AP Computer Science course that I taught. The class was intended to be comparable to a first year course offered in colleges and universities, and covered topics that would normally comprise six or more semester hours of college level computer science coursework. The course was intended to serve both as an introductory course for computer science majors and as a substantial service course for people who will major in other disciplines that require significant involvement with computing.

Buck, T. L. (2009). *Curriculum Development, Assessment and Design*. Retrieved from: http://www.rubrics4assessment.net/curriculum.htm

Author's Description: During the 2000-2001 academic year at Marshall School, Duluth, as part of the Teacher Assessment Committee, I conducted a literature review of current research, as well as local, state, and national teacher and instruction assessment tools and standards. Throughout the course of the 2000-2001 school year, I gathered and archived many useful research based systems for evaluating curricula, instructors, and students.

Since initially constructing this website in 2002, its goal has continued to be to share some of these authentic assessment tools, to describe the assessment techniques that I have adopted, and to provide learning and assessment resources designed especially with these objectives in mind.

Buck, T. L. (2004). *Learning Styles and Web-based Learning: An investigation of field dependence - independence and cognitive abilities in a nonlinear distance learning environment*. Dissertation, Walden University.

Abstract: This study was designed to identify how field dependence-independence learners differ, and how dominant mediation or cognitive abilities differ, in performance, completion rates, navigation styles, and a sense of "becoming lost" in a secondary education non-linear hypertext modular distance learning environment. A total of 149 secondary education AP English students registered, were tracked over a four-week period, and completed all necessary parts of the course module to be included in this study. The population of high school students studied was a non-random opportunity sample. Multiple measures of subject performance, demographics, and situational factors were made by means of Web-based surveys, Embedded Figures Test (EFT), Gregorc Style Delineator (GSD), instructional lessons, and examinations. The registrant sample was predominately seventeen years old, female, living and attending high school in an urban city in Northern Minnesota, or Wisconsin.

This study revealed that between the Field Dependence (FD) and the Field Independence (FI) learners, as defined by the EFT, there were no significant differences in the group means for module quizzes or module scores, in the group count for module completion/non-completion, nor in either their navigation styles, or in there being a sense of "becoming lost." Additionally, similar results were found between the dominant cognitive ability groups, as defined by the GSD, of Concrete Sequential (CS), Concrete Random (CR), Abstract Sequential (AS), and Abstract Random (AR). This suggests that a non-linear hypertext modular curriculum provides sufficient flexibility in construction and presentation, allowing diverse learning styles to become less of an influencing factor in performance, completion rates, navigation styles, or students developing a sense of "becoming lost." Recommendations for future research include further research of other demographic groups of students (e.g., at-risk, learning disabled, average students, different age groups, socio-economic factors, various ethnic groups, etc.), and correlations with other cognitive instruments examining age, educational attainment levels, and gender based patterns.

Burden, P. & Byrd, D. (2012). *Methods for effective teaching*. New Jersey, NY: Pearson Publishing.

Book Description: The sixth edition of Methods for Effective Teaching provides the most current research-based coverage of teaching methods for K-12 classrooms on the market today. In a straightforward, user-friendly tone, the expert author team writes to prepare current and future educators to be effective in meeting the needs of all the students they teach. In this new edition, all content is carefully aligned to professional standards, including the recently revised InTASC standards. Uniquely emphasizing today's contemporary issues, such as both teacher-centered and student-centered strategies; a myriad of ways to differentiate instruction, promote student thinking, and actively engage students in learning; approaches for teaching English language learners, and an added emphasis on culturally responsive teaching, this highly-regarded textbook is the perfect combination of sound teaching methods and cutting edge content.

Chandra and Lloyd (2008). The Methodological Nettle: ICT and Student Achievement. *British Journal of Educational Technology*, *v*39 n6, 1087-1098.

Abstract: A major challenge for researchers and educators has been to discern the effect of ICT use on student learning outcomes. This paper maps the achievements in Year 10 Science of two cohorts of students over two years where students in the first year studied in a traditional environment while students in the second took part in a blended or e-Learning environment. Using both quantitative and qualitative methods, the authors have shown that ICT, through an e-Learning intervention, did improve student performance in terms of test scores. They have also shown that this improvement was not global with the results for previously high-performing female students tending to fall while the results for lower-achieving boys rose. There was also a seeming mismatch between some students' affective responses to the new environment and their test scores. This study shows the complexity of ICT-mediated environments through its identification and description of three core issues which beset the credibility of research in ICT in education. These are (a) ICT as an agent of learning, (b) site specificity, and (c) global improvement.

Churches, A. (2008). *Data Analysis - Bloom's Digital Taxonomy Rubric.* Retrieved from:

edorigami.wikispaces.com/file/view/data+analysis+rubric.pdf

Author's Description: This is a rubric for data processing, manipulation, presentation and analysis. The rubric is designed for students taking raw data and suitably entering this into a spreadsheet (data processing). The processed data is then manipulated to add value using features like sort, filter, formula and equations. The manipulated data is presented in a suitable format or formats to enable analysis. Students are able to select suitable charts for the data types and suitably label tables, titles, axes, labels and keys. Students can then make accurate analysis of the data and trends, with an awareness of errors and inaccuracies.

Condie, R & Livingston, K. (2007). Blending online learning with traditional approaches: changing practices. *British Journal of Educational Technology*, 38/2, 337–348.

Abstract: Considerable claims have been made for the development of e-Learning, either as stand-alone programs or alongside more traditional approaches to teaching and learning, for students across school and tertiary education. National initiatives have improved the position of schools in terms of access to hardware and electronic networking, software and educational resources, and staff development. The potential of e-Learning to improve learning and teaching, and in turn, attainment, may be contested by academics but the policy makers are generally positive. Many countries across Europe and North America have adopted information and communication technology (ICT) as a central plank in school improvement and effectiveness planning. At the centre, however, remain the teacher and the learner. The impact of ICT on the learning experience will depend upon the roles adopted by each, the model of the learner held by the teacher and the pedagogy adopted. This paper considers the ways in which teachers and students responded to the implementation of one particular online program and considers the approaches adopted and the attitudes to its use. The SCHOLAR program is designed to complement rather than replace traditional teaching and learning approaches within schools and is aimed at students in the post-compulsory years of secondary school working towards external certification. It has a number of features including course materials, revision exercises, self-assessment facilities and a discussion forum. The independent evaluation of SCHOLAR looked at the impact that its use made on learning and teaching in the post-16 classroom and the differing ways in which teachers and students used the various elements of the program. While it did appear to have a positive impact on attainment, the evidence indicates that this might have been greater had the teachers modified their practice, blending learning through SCHOLAR with more traditional methods.

Demetriou, A. (1998). Nooplasis: 10 + 1 Postulates about the Formation of Mind. *Learning and Instruction, v*8 n4, 271-87.

Abstract: Outlines a general model about the dynamic organization and development of the mind and draws the implications of this model for learning and instruction by presenting 10 postulates about the organization of the mind and 1 general postulate about the dynamic relations between systems of the mind and the mind and education.

Dubuclet, K. S. (2008). *Teaching Presence: A Focus on the Instructor's Role in Online Collaborative Learning*. Dissertation: Louisiana State University, Baton Rouge.

Abstract: The use of e-Learning has been extended beyond simply providing access to information to providing the ability to learn collaboratively via an interactive learning environment. The ability to create an online collaborative and interactive environment is a challenge. This study strove to examine the most effective design and facilitative strategies for fostering student learning and participation in hopes to make design and implementation of online discussions easier and more efficient for teachers. The primary goal of this study was to understand how the degree of instructor presence influenced students' perception of learning and how students engaged in deeper levels of learning in an online collaborative learning environment. More specifically, the study explored the relationship between design and facilitative strategies in online discussions and student participation, student learning, and students' perceptions of their online learning experience. An embedded, multiple-case study design was used. Three completely online classes taught by the same instructor were chosen for this study (n = 55). During the Fall 2007 semester, data were collected from observations, discussion transcripts, teacher interviews, student surveys and student grades. Quantitative data included student responses on a perception survey, final course grades, and the frequency of discussion posts. Qualitative data included on-going observations, on-going teacher interviews, open-ended questions on a student perception survey, and discussion transcripts. Results showed that the teacher's role in online discussions is influential to student participation and learning. More specifically, certain strategies such as participation requirements and question design were related to an increase in participation and learning. Factors such as addressing students by name, providing immediate feedback, providing on-going communication, and providing individual attention may have also contributed to student learning. The findings of this research are consistent with that of previous studies. Consequently, they add merit to the importance of teacher presence in online learning, particularly in the areas of course structure and question design. Implications for practice are discussed.

Elliott, S. N. (1995). Creating meaningful performance assessments. *ERIC Digest E531*. EDRS no: ED381985.

Abstract: This digest offers principles of performance assessment as an alternative to norm-referenced tests. The definition of performance assessment developed by the U.S. Congress's Office of Technology and Assessment is given, common features are listed, and the terms "performance" and "authentic" are defined. Suggested guidelines for addressing validity in performance assessments focus on internal characteristics of the assessment, the relationship of the measure to similar measures or future performance, and the intended effects of using the instrument. In providing evidence for the reliability and validity of performance assessment, evaluators are urged to address: (1) assessment as a curriculum event; (2) task content alignment with curriculum; (3) scoring and subsequent communications with consumers; and (4) linking and comparing results over time. Teachers are urged to use performance assessments in ways which will interact with instruction.

Garrison, D. R., Anderson, T., & Archer, W. (2000). Critical Inquiry in a text-based environment: computer conferencing in higher education. *The Internet and Higher Education, 2(2-3)*, 87-105.

Abstract: The purpose of this study is to provide conceptual order and a tool for the use of computer-mediated communication (CMC) and computer conferencing in supporting an educational experience. Central to the study introduced here is a model of community inquiry that constitutes three elements essential to an educational transaction—cognitive presence, social presence, and teaching presence. Indicators (key words/phrases) for each of the three elements emerged from the analysis of computer-conferencing transcripts. The indicators described represent a template or tool for researchers to analyze written transcripts, as well as a guide to educators for the optimal use of computer conferencing as a medium to facilitate an educational transaction. This research would suggest that computer conferencing has considerable potential to create a community of inquiry for educational purposes.

Garrison, D. R., & Arbaugh J. B. (2007). Researching the community of inquiry framework: Review, issues, and future directions. *The Internet and Higher Education, 10,* 157-172.

Abstract: Since its publication in The Internet and Higher Education, Garrison, Anderson, and Archer's [Garrison, D. R., Anderson, T., & Archer, W. (2000). Critical inquiry in a text-based environment: Computer conferencing in higher education. The Internet and Higher Education, 2(2–3), 87–105.] community of inquiry (CoI) framework has generated substantial interest among online learning researchers. This literature review examines recent research pertaining to the overall framework as well as to specific studies on social, teaching, and cognitive presence. We then use the findings from this literature to identify potential future directions for research. Some of these research directions include the need for more quantitatively-oriented studies, the need for more cross-disciplinary studies, and the opportunities for identifying factors that moderate and/or extend the relationship between the framework's components and online course outcomes.

Garrison, D. & Shale, D. (1987). Mapping the boundaries of distance education: Problems in defining the field. *The American Journal of Distance Education* (1), 4-13.

Abstract: An audioteleconferencing system enhanced with a microcomputer-based telewriting system was used for the delivery of an introductory statistics course designed for home study which was offered by Athabasca University. From the instructor's point of view, the telewriter system made supporting the delivery of the statistics course much easier and more convenient than was possible by using either the telephone or teleconferencing alone. However, a number of technical problems with the telewriter system were cited by all students as a major problem throughout the project. Instructionally, the students were dissatisfied with the lecture style of presentation used by the instructor and with the rate of pacing used to cover the course content. Students particularly questioned the reproduction of material given in the text and student manual. In fact, many felt that they could progress as well reading the material on their own, at home, and to a large degree this would account for the substantial fall-off in attendance at sessions at the six study sites, and the termination of the course with a 67% completion rate. Students indicated that two of their initial expectations for the course--personal contact with the instructor and personal contact with other students--were not met. Possible explanations for the overall negative assessments of this course include a negative reaction to the instructor and the associated instructional style, the technical problems experienced, and the nature of the subject matter.

Gentile, M. J. (2007). Authentic assessment of scientific ability, *The Internet and Higher Education, 10*(3), 202-209.

Abstract: Effective science teaching at the undergraduate level requires that faculty learn and adopt effective instructional practices as well as methods for the active assessment of student learning. Yet, formal training in learner-centered instruction and assessment is seldom part of the preparation science faculty receive prior to entering the undergraduate classroom. Faculty development in learning assessment can enhance the effectiveness of efforts to reform science education, and it is a crucial component of institutional capacity for science education reform.

Goertzen, P., & Sir Kristjansson, C. (2007). Interpersonal dimensions of community in graduate online learning: Exploring social presence through the lens of Systemic Functional Linguistics, *The Internet and Higher Education, 10*(3), 212-230.

Abstract: This exploratory case study considers the interpersonal dimension of collaborative learning in an online graduate community that is based on a cohort approach to education which is characterized by the social construction of knowledge. Discourse data from two graduate courses are analyzed for interpersonal elements associated with social presence through the lens of Systemic Functional Linguistics. A general profile of the interpersonal dimension of the learning community is provided along with a consideration of cognitive engagement and the interpersonal dynamics of two dilemmatic situations. Data analyses indicate that social presence is much more than social chat and that the nature of the collaborative learning process is deeply intertwined with interpersonal engagement among participants.

Hale, J. A. (2008). *A guide to curriculum mapping: Planning, implementing, and sustaining the process*. Thousand Oaks, CA: Corwin Press.

Book Description: This practical, step-by-step guide examines the stages of contemplating, planning, and implementing curriculum mapping initiatives that can improve student learning and create sustainable change.

Harlow, L. L., Burkholder, G. J, Morrow, J. A. (2006). Engaging Students in Learning: An Application with Quantitative Psychology. *Teaching of Psychology*, v33 n4 p231-235.

Abstract: In response to calls for more engaging and interactive pedagogy, we simultaneously implemented 4 rousing learning activities: peer-mentored learning, student reports of what was clear (or not) from a previous lecture, consult corners where student groups provided course-informed solutions to problem-based scenarios, and applied projects presented to the class. Students in several sections of a quantitative psychology course responded positively, reporting significantly less anxiety and greater self-efficacy regarding quantitative topics at the end of the semester compared to the beginning. We provide suggestions for applying these learning activities to other psychology courses.

Hart, P. M., & Rowley, J. B. (1996). How Video Case Studies Can Promote Reflective Dialogue. *Educational Leadership*, v53 n6 p28-29

Abstract: Inspired by Donald Schon's work "Educating the Reflective Practitioner" (1987), the authors create virtual worlds using an approach combining video technology and the case teaching method. This article describes two video series, "Mentoring the New Teacher" and "Becoming a Star Urban Teacher," aimed at enhancing the growth of teachers as reflective practitioners.

Henderson, T. (1997). *Multimedia Handbook of Engaged Learning Projects*. Glenview, IL: North Central Regional Educational Laboratory.

Handbook Description: The field of multimedia learning has emerged as a coherent discipline with an accumulated research base that has never been synthesized and organized. This reference constitutes an original work devoted to comprehensive coverage of research and theory in the field of multimedia learning. It focuses on how people learn from words and pictures in computer-based environments. Multimedia environments include online instructional presentations, interactive lessons, e-courses, simulation Games, virtual reality, and computer-supported, in-class presentations.

Jacobs, H. H. (1997). *Mapping the big picture: Integrating curriculum and assessment K-12*. Alexandria, VA: Association for Supervision and Curriculum Development.

Publisher's Description: Teachers have always used the school calendar to plan instruction. Now, using a standard computer word-processing program, they can collect real-time information about what is actually taught to create "curriculum maps." These maps provide a clear picture of what is happening in their classes at specific points during the school year. The benefits of this kind of mapping are obvious for integrating curriculum: when curriculum maps are developed for every grade level, educators see not only the details of each map, but also the "big picture" for that school or district. They can see where subjects already come together--and where they don't, but probably should. In Mapping the Big Picture, Heidi Hayes Jacobs describes a seven-step process for creating and working with curriculum maps, from data collection to ongoing curriculum review. She discusses the importance of asking "essential questions" and of designing assessments that reflect what teachers know about the students in their care. She also offers a viable alternative to the "curriculum committees" that are part of almost every school district in the United States. The book concludes with more than 20 sample curriculum maps from real schools, all of which were developed using the process described in this book.

Jacobs, H .H. (2004). *Getting results with curriculum mapping.* Alexandria, VA: Association for Supervision and Curriculum Development.

Publisher's Description: Curriculum maps are among the simplest yet most effective tools for improving teaching and learning. Because they require people to draw explicit connections between content, skills, and assessment measures, these maps help ensure that all aspects of a lesson are aligned not only with each other, but also with mandated standards and tests. In Getting Results with Curriculum Mapping, Heidi Hayes Jacobs and her coauthors offer a wide range of perspectives on how to get the most out of the curriculum mapping process in districts and schools. In addition to detailed examples of maps from schools across the United States, the authors offer concrete advice on such critical issues as:
- Preparing educators to implement mapping procedures,
- Using software to create unique mapping databases,
- Integrating decision-making structures and staff development initiatives through mapping,
- Helping school communities adjust to new curriculum review processes, and
- Making mapping an integral part of literacy training.

Teachers, administrators, staff developers, and policymakers alike will find this book an essential guide to curriculum mapping and a vital resource for spearheading school improvement efforts.

Jacobs, H. H. (2006). *Active literacy across the curriculum: Strategies for reading, writing, speaking, and listening*, Larchmont, NY: Eye On Education.

Publisher's Description: Highly acclaimed author Heidi Hayes Jacobs shows teachers – at very grade level and in every subject area -- how to integrate the teaching of literacy skills into their daily curriculum. With an emphasis on school wide collaborative planning, she shows how curriculum mapping sustains literacy between grade levels and subjects.

Jacobs, H. H. (2010). *Curriculum 21: Essential education for a changing world*. Alexandria, VA: Association for Supervision and Curriculum Development.

Publisher's Description: What year are you preparing your students for? 1973? 1995? Can you honestly say that your school s curriculum and the program you use are preparing your students for 2015 or 2020? Are you even preparing them for today? With those provocative questions, author and educator Heidi Hayes Jacobs launches a powerful case for overhauling, updating, and injecting life into the K 12 curriculum. Sharing her expertise as a world-renowned curriculum designer and calling upon the collective wisdom of 10 education thought leaders, Jacobs provides insight and inspiration in the following key areas:

- Content and assessment--How to identify what to keep, what to cut, and what to create, and where portfolios and other new kinds of assessment fit into the picture.
- Program structures--How to improve our use of time and space and groupings of students and staff.
- Technology--How it s transforming teaching, and how to take advantage of students natural facility with technology.
- Media literacy--The essential issues to address, and the best resources for helping students become informed users of multiple forms of media.
- Globalization--What steps to take to help students gain a global perspective.
- Sustainability--How to instill enduring values and beliefs that will lead to healthier local, national, and global communities.
- Habits of mind--The thinking habits that students, teachers, and administrators need to develop and practice to succeed in school, work, and life.

The answers to these questions and many more make Curriculum 21 the ideal guide for transforming our schools into what they must become: learning organizations that match the times in which we live.

Jacobs, H. H. & Johnson, A. J. (2009). *The curriculum mapping planner: Templates, tools, and resources for effective professional development.* Alexandria, VA: Association for Supervision and Curriculum Development.

> Publisher's Description: Curriculum mapping is a powerful tool for school improvement, but moving into mapping requires a genuine paradigm shift. Perhaps you've tried curriculum mapping in your school or district, but you've never found a way to get the most out of it. Or perhaps you've introduced teachers to curriculum mapping but are unsure of the next steps to ensure lasting change. Heidi Hayes Jacobs and Ann Johnson have designed The Curriculum Mapping Planner to help schools deliver effective training in curriculum mapping. The planner describes a four-phase professional development program composed of 12 modules, which are presented as 12 curriculum maps for professional development. In short, this book will help you map mapping. Each module s curriculum map includes possible follow-up assignments and resources. The assignments can provide practice for the participants, help them maintain focus on curriculum mapping, and help set the stage and prepare them for the next training session. The resources provide additional information and can be used in the study groups or as a support for the activities. And an online component containing sample curriculum maps, templates, and handouts makes it easy to organize and distribute materials to participants. With the systematic approach presented in this planner, staff developers, teacher leaders, and administrators can work successfully together to create a curriculum that truly challenges and supports all students.

Jonassen, D. H. (1992). Learner-Generated vs. Instructor-Provided Analysis of Semantic Relationships. *Journal of Computing in Higher Education, v*4 n2, 12-42.

> Abstract: This study explores the effectiveness of an instructional strategy which displays appropriate knowledge structures versus a learning strategy that engages learners in defining knowledge structures by comparing the effects of providing graphical organizers in the form of completed frames with requiring students to complete frames as a study strategy prior to examinations. The learning variable being investigated is structural knowledge, i.e., the knowledge of how concepts within a domain are interrelated. The subjects were 56 students from a general psychology course at a large community college in Denver, Colorado, who were divided into two groups. Three subject-matter exams were designed to test recall of the text and lecture material, and subscales were developed to measure three aspects of structural knowledge: relationship proximity judgments, semantic relationships, and analogies. Students were also asked to complete a questionnaire assessing the extent of use and helpfulness of the instructor-provided and student-generated maps. Analyses of the data

showed that both groups improved their relationship knowledge by focusing on the relationships when using the instructor-provided graphic organizers, and structural knowledge acquisition improved significantly. Between the second and third exams, however, an apparent task-by-group interaction occurred as Group 1 relationship scores appear to have benefited more from the learning strategy than Group 2 scores. Factors that may have influenced the results include the treatment, the content or test difficulties, and the difficulty of the mapping exercise.

Jones, T. (2002). Options and Considerations for Distance Education: Learner Assessment and Self-assessment, (3)3. TOJDE (*Turkish Online Journal of Distance Education*). ISSN 1302-6488 Available at: http://tojde.anadolu.edu.tr/tojde7/articles/Jonestxt.htm

Author's Description: The explosion in distance education programs and the associated course offerings that has resulted from the accessibility and reliability of the Internet has moved distance education professionals to reconsider a number of program components. These have ranged from instructional systems (design) to level of program (diploma, high school, university) to administration (registration, fees, scheduling) and to faculty (full-time, part-time, student supervision). One component of distance-delivered programs that can particularly problematic is the evaluation or assessment of learner achievement for, in the final analysis, modifications to existing delivery models (face-to-face, dual and single mode institutions), no matter how innovative and effective, must still be held accountable for the integrity, reliability and validity of the assessment procedures of the learners.

Juul, J. (2003). The game, the player, the world: looking for a heart of gameness, in: Marinka Copier and Joost Raessens (eds) *Level Up: Digital Games Research Conference Proceedings*. Utrecht: Universiteit Utrecht, 2003.

Abstract: This paper proposes a definition of games and describes the classic game model, a list of six features that are necessary and sufficient for something to be a game. The definition shows games to be transmedial: *There is no single game medium, but rather a number of game media, each with its own strengths*. The computer is simply the latest game medium to emerge. While computer games1 are therefore part of the broader area of games, they have in many cases evolved beyond the classic game model.

Keegan, D. (1996). Interaction and communication, (Chapter 6, pp.89-107). In Keegan, D., The foundations of distance education. Kent, UK.: Croom Helm..

Book Description: Distance education and training provision has expanded dramatically over the past few years. This best-selling introduction to the field has helped many to understand the origins and background of distance education, and has been used by students and professionals as a guide to policy and practice. It has now been updated in the light of the developments in recent years in Eastern Europe and the enormous advances in the use of new technologies. A new case study of distance education in China is also included.

Khan, K. S., Davies, D. A., & Gupta, J. K. (2001). Formative Self-Assessment Using Multiple True-False Questions on the Internet: Feedback According to Confidence About Correct Knowledge. *Medical Teacher, v*23 n2, 158-163.

Abstract: Introduces a Web-based formative assessment system that consists of knowledge tests based on multiple true-false questions which is capable of monitoring students' educational progress on an individual basis or as small groups and providing feedback.

Kolowich, S. (2011). Blackboard's Next Phase. *Inside Higher Ed. 18*(3), 9-12.

Abstract: Examines and discusses how close to 95 percent of institutions had some learning management system in place, according to the Campus Computing Project. Accordingly, Blackboard's business strategy is changing: with the company adding four new, separately licensed products to its menu in the last three years, Blackboard expects that it will soon no longer rely on Learn, its popular learning management system, as its main engine.

Borich (2008). Letting Students Shape Instructional Strategies. *Learning Languages, v*14 n1, 22-24.

Abstract: When the author was teaching in an elementary foreign language exposure (FLEX) program several years ago, she completed a research project that documented student learning gained from student dialogue journals. The action research initiative taught her the value of being reflective about her teaching practices. Her thesis research requirements forced her to carefully collect, analyze and reflect on student journals, rubrics and authentic assessment tools. In doing so, the author learned which teaching strategies made a difference. By using this evaluation process of reflecting on professional practice based on authentic assessment, learning community leaders could help teachers teach more effectively.

Lyle, V. (2006) *Leadership for curriculum mapping*. Unpublished Manuscript. Marion School District #2, Marion, Illinois.

Guide Description: This UCEA resource was produced as part of a commitment by UCEA to develop and share resources on effective educational leadership preparation. The guide draws on extensive evaluation research and program development experience as well as the collective efforts of the field to date.

Mager, R. F. (2005). *Preparing Instructional Objectives*. Belmont, Calif.: Fearon.

Book Description: Offers a program on how to identify, select and write specific objectives to be achieved by instruction and provides guided practice for the lecturer or course designer through exercises and case studies.

McGonigal, J. (2011). *Reality is Broken. Why Games Make Us Better and How They Can Change the World.* New York, NY: Penguin Press (USA) Inc.

Book Description: With 174 million gamers in the United States alone, we now live in a world where every generation will be a gamer generation. But why, Jane McGonigal asks, should games be used for escapist entertainment alone? In this groundbreaking book, she shows how we can leverage the power of games to fix what is wrong with the real world-from social problems like depression and obesity to global issues like poverty and climate change-and introduces us to cutting-edge games that are already changing the business, education, and nonprofit worlds. Written for gamers and non-gamers alike, Reality Is Broken shows that the future will belong to those who can understand, design, and play games.

Michael, D. & Chen, S. (2005). *Proof of learning: assessment in serious games.* Available online:

http://www.gamasutra.com/view/feature/2433/proof_of_learning_assessment_in_.php.

Conclusion: "The future of serious games as an educational tool depends on their improved support for completion assessment, in-process assessment, and teacher evaluation. Designers and developers will need to reach beyond simple multiple-choice questions and incorporate the best of video game tutorials with sound educational and psychometric techniques.

Moreover, if game developers can show skeptical teachers that not only do serious games help teach the material better, but that the games can be easily integrated into existing lesson plans, those teachers are bound to lose their objections.

"[Serious games] will not grow as an industry unless the learning experience is definable, quantifiable and measurable," Corti says. "Assessment is the future of serious games."" (Michael & Chen, 2005).

Mueller, Jon (2011). *Authentic Assessment Toolbox* [online document]. Available online: http://jonathan.mueller.faculty.noctrl.edu/toolbox/

Description: Authentic Assessment Toolbox, a how-to text on creating authentic tasks, rubrics, and standards for measuring and improving student learning.

Montgomery, K. (2001). *Authentic assessment: A guide for elementary teachers*. New York: Longman.

Book Description: This brief guide offers pre-service and in-service elementary teachers a simple introduction to the concepts and best practices in authentic assessment. The text offers a child-centered approach of assessment that promotes the belief students should become self-regulated, lifelong learners. It clearly defines authentic assessment terminology and techniques and provides field-tested tools and strategies for assessing all children. The research and practice passed the stringent tests of hundreds of practicing elementary teachers. Boxed Features explicitly illustrate assessment concepts and examples. For elementary teachers.

Perraton, H. (1988). *A theory for distance education*. In Distance education: International perspectives, ed. D. Sewart, D. Keegan, and B. Holmberg, 34-45. New York: Routledge.

Book Description: Chronicles the great change in distance education, presenting the best writings on the subject published during the last ten years. This book should be of interest to teachers and students of distance and comparative education.

Piccoli, G., Ahmad, R., & Ives, B. (2001). Web-based virtual learning environments: A research framework and a preliminary assessment of effectiveness in basic it skills training. *MIS Quarterly*, 25, 4, 401-426.

Abstract: An empirical analysis was conducted to compare Face-to-Face learning to three formats of online learning: hybrid, asynchronous, and synchronous. Student satisfaction was used as a surrogate to measure success in learning environments. Over 200 students from eight disciplines took part in a university wide study. The study found no significant difference in student satisfaction among the four learning environments. Directions for future research were proposed.

Raza, A., & Murad, H. S. (2008). Knowledge Democracy and the Implications to Information Access. Multicultural Education & Technology Journal, v2 n1, 37-46.

Abstract: The purpose of this paper is to examine the concept of "knowledge democracy," deploying a pluralistic, and cross disciplinary and humanistic critique. Design/methodology/approach: This is a culturally pluralistic and humanistic interpretation of globally emergent form of learning pedagogy, particularly manifested in e-Learning. Findings: This paper explores the concept of knowledge democracy in the context of knowledge and information revolution. It has been argued that knowledge democratization implies freedom and equality to access information and knowledge across cultures and societies, particularly in the context of globalization. It is asserted that a democratization of the notion of knowledge would cause a paradigm shift; the way instruction and education are socially structured in different social systems. The knowledge society provides a new spirit of global sharing of values, acceptance of others and learning to live with divergent worldviews. It is contended that e-Learning in particular sets a new global social opportunity to transcend regional, racial and national prejudices. Originality/value: The paper underscores the significance of pluralistic and humanistic perspective on knowledge and e-Learning.

Richardson, J. C., & Ice, P. (2010). Investigating students level of critical thinking, across instructional strategies in online discussions. *Internet and Higher Education, 13(1-2)*, 52 - 59.

Abstract: Online discussion questions, which reflect differing instructional strategies, can take many forms and it is important for designers and instructors to understand how the various strategies can impact students' critical thinking levels. For the purpose of the study three instructional strategies used in the development and implementation of online discussion questions were examined: a case-based discussion, a debate, and an open-ended (or topical) discussion. Using a mixed method approach, the study focused on critical thinking levels as described in the Community of Inquiry (CoI) framework and operationalized in the Practical Inquiry Model (PIM). The study investigated (1) participants' preferred instructional strategy and rationales for the selection, (2) the contribution of student background and demographic criteria to students' preferred instructional strategy, (3) the contribution of students' strategy preferences in predicting level of critical thinking, based on the Practical Inquiry Model's (PIM) indicators, and (4) comparisons of participants' critical thinking levels across instructional strategies. Implications for the design of online discussions that foster critical thinking are discussed.

Richey, R. C., Klein, J. D. (2007). *Design and Development Research*. Mahwah, New Jersey: Lawrence Erlbatun Associates, Publishers.

Book Description: Design and Development Research thoroughly discusses methods and strategies appropriate for conducting design and development research. Rich with examples and explanations, the book describes actual strategies that researchers have used to conduct two major types of design and development research: 1) product and tool research

and 2) model research. Common challenges confronted by researchers in the field when planning and conducting a study are explored and procedural explanations are supported by a wide variety of examples taken from current literature. Samples of actual research tools are also presented. Important features in this volume include:
- concise checklists at the end of each chapter to give a clear summary of the steps involved in the various phases of a project;
- an examination of the critical types of information and data often gathered in studies, and unique procedures for collecting these data;
- examples of data collection instruments, as well as the use of technology in data collection; and
- a discussion of the process of extracting meaning from data and interpreting product and tool and model research findings.

Design and Development Research is appropriate for both experienced researchers and those preparing to become researchers. It is intended for scholars interested in planning and conducting design and development research, and is intended to stimulate future thinking about methods, strategies, and issues related to the field.

Ryan, C. D. (2004). *Authentic Assessment A Professional's Guide*. Westminster, CA: Teacher Created Materials, Inc.

Book Description: Using material from 130 educators and 3,000 students from 24 "restructured" elementary, middle and high schools nationwide, this guide presents: * A rationale for the importance of students constructing knowledge, through disciplined inquiry, to produce discourse and performance that has value and meaning beyond school ; *A set of integrated standards for analyzing teaching, assessment practice and student performance according to this rationale ; * Examples of teachers lessons, assessment tasks, and student performance which succeed on the standards ; * Specific rubrics and scoring rules for applying the standards in elementary, middle and high schools. This guide is intended to stimulate teacher reflection on standards for authentic intellectual quality, with the ultimate goal of helping teachers develop more authentic instruction, assessment and student performance. It includes scenarios and general guidelines for adapting the standards to the needs of particular schools, grade levels, and subjects.

Shea, P., S: Bidjerano, T. (2009). Community of inquiry as a theoretical framework to foster "epistemic engagement" and "cognitive presence" in online education. *Computers & Education*, 52(3), 543 - 553.

Abstract: In this paper, several recent theoretical conceptions of technology-mediated education are examined and a study of 2159 online learners is presented. The study validates an instrument designed to measure teaching, social, and cognitive presence indicative of a community of learners within the community of inquiry (CoI) framework [Garrison, D. R., Anderson, T., & Archer, W. (2000). Critical inquiry in a text-based environment: Computer conferencing in higher education. "The Internet and Higher Education," 2, 1-19; Garrison, D. R., Anderson, T., & Archer, W. (2001). Critical thinking, cognitive presence, and computer conferencing in distance education. "American Journal of Distance Education," 15(1), 7-23]. Results indicate that the survey items cohere into interpretable factors that represent the intended constructs. Further it was determined through structural equation modeling that 70% of the variance in the online students' levels of cognitive presence, a multivariate measure of learning, can be modeled based on their reports of their instructors' skills in fostering teaching presence and their own abilities to establish a sense of social presence. Additional analysis identifies more details of the relationship between learner understandings of teaching and social presence and its impact on their cognitive presence. Implications for online teaching, policy, and faculty development are discussed.

Simonson M., Smaldino, S, Albright, M. and Zvacek, S. (2011). *Assessment for distance education* (ch 11). In Teaching and Learning at a Distance: Foundations of Distance Education. Upper Saddle River, NJ: Prentice-Hall.

Book Description: Teaching and Learning at a Distance: Foundations of Distance Education, Fifth Edition, provides its readers with the most comprehensive coverage on the market today of information about distance education in the 21st century. Primarily written for pre-service teachers, corporate trainers, and staff development programs that discuss teaching distant learners or managing distance education systems. Readers will be better equipped with the knowledge and ability to select appropriate strategies for teaching the distant learner and how to implement this new knowledge in a distance learning program, so important to today's educational culture. Five over-arching themes support the text: 1) defining distance education, 2) the importance of research development, 3) distance learning is a viable and increasingly important alternative for teaching and learning, 4) equivalency theory, and 5) the book should be comprehensive—which means it should cover as much as is possible of the various ways instruction is made available to distant learners. Significantly revised and updated, the fifth edition now includes these noteworthy new features and more: chapter goals and objectives, chapter discussion questions, a look at best practice issues, new strategies and techniques, over thirty-percent new resources and references, and a stronger emphasis on how to design, deliver, and evaluate online instruction.

Sparks. D. (2003). Interview with Michael Fullan. *Journal of Staff Development*, v24(1).

Overview: In this interview Canadian educational researcher, Michael Fullan, explores the links between instructional leadership, school culture, and change. He describes features of professional learning communities that promote change and how to embed change in practice. He also discusses the effects of school culture on change and how to raise the quality of that culture. The importance of relationships to learning and the need to foster independence to be flexible in meeting problems are explained. He describes five key features of leaders and the importance of moral purpose. Fullan has written extensively on leadership and change and has worked in collaborative relationships to bring about change in schools.

Steinkuehler, C., Squire, K., & Barab, S. (2012). *Games, Learning, and Society: Learning and Meaning in the Digital Age (Learning in Doing: Social, Cognitive and Computational Perspectives)*. New York, NY: Cambridge University Press.

Book Description: This volume covers major topics in the field of videogames and learning, including game design, game culture, and games as a tool for teaching and learning. The chapters are written by some of the most influential thinkers, designers, and writers in the field. Together, their work functions both as an excellent introduction to the field and proof that videogames are an important medium for shaping how people - young and old alike - think and learn in the digital age.

Stevens, K. (2005). Rural schools as regional centers of e-Learning and the management of digital knowledge: The case of Newfoundland and Labrador. In International Journal of Education and Development using Information and Communication Technology. *IJEDICT*, v2 (4): 119-127.

Abstract: Changes to traditional learning environments needed to be made because the creation of electronic learning environments effectively broke down barriers of space and distance, and required teachers to work more collaboratively often across learning sites (which were traditional classroom environments).

Tarouco, L. & Hack, L. (2001). New tools for assessment in distance education [online document]. Available online:

http://www.pgie.ufrgs.br/Webfolioead/artigo1.html

Abstract: This paper describes a strategy for improving the quality of distance education assessment providing a set of complementary tools to help on formative evaluation. Regular forms to assess learning are analyzed and Kirkpatrick's model for evaluation is described as well as a set of tools to provide capability to asses according this model. The set of complementary tools includes consensus, tracking, voting and self-evaluation

Tracey, M. W., & Richey R. C. (2007). ID model construction and validation: a multiple intelligences case. *Educational Technology Research and Development, 55(4)*, 369-390.

Abstract: This is a report of a developmental research study that aimed to construct and validate an instructional design (ID) model that incorporates the theory and practice of multiple intelligences (MI). The study consisted of three phases. In phase one, the theoretical foundations of multiple Intelligences and ID were examined to guide the development of such model. In phase two the model components were determined and an initial model was constructed. In phase three, the model was reviewed and validated by experts in the field of ID through a three-round Delphi study. The result was a revised and validated Multiple Intelligences Design Model. This paper presents the decision-making processes and procedures used in model development, and provides a framework for the internal validation of ID models using expert review procedures.

Udelofen, S. (2005). *Keys to curriculum mapping: strategies and tools to make it work*. Thousand Oaks, CA: Corwin Press.

Book Description: Packed with templates, flowcharts, tips, and troubleshooting techniques for curriculum mapping, this practical resource provides the tools necessary for successful implementation and exciting results.

Visscher-Voerman, I., & Gustafson, K. L. (2004). Paradigm in the theory and practice of education and training design. *Educational Technology, Research and Development, 52(2)*, 69-89.

Abstract: Over the years, many authors have tried to describe, conceptualize, and visualize the instructional design or development processes via a variety of process models. Most descriptions imply a rather homogeneous view of design, depicting it as an overall problem-solving process following general phases such as analysis, design and development, implementation, and evaluation (ADDIE). However, researchers who have investigated how instructional designers actually work suggest that the process is much more heterogeneous and diverse than these ADDIE models suggest. This study collected case study data from 24 instructional designers in six different settings; they were identified as experts by their peers. The design processes they used for a specific project were compared to four different paradigms created from the literature. The four paradigms and their underlying theoretical foundations are described and illustrated. Detailed results are reported, and reasons that designers did or did not use a particular paradigm are considered.

Vanchar, S. C., South, J. B., Williams, D. D., Allen. S., Wilson, B. G. (2010). Struggling with theory? A qualitative investigation of conceptual tool use in instructional design. *Educational Technology Research Development 58*(1), 39 - 60.

Abstract: This study employed a qualitative research design to investigate instructional designers' views and uses of conceptual tools in design work (e.g., learning theories and design theories). While past research has examined how instructional designers spend their time, how they generally make decisions, and expert-novice differences, little attention has been paid to the value and perceptions of conceptual tools, from the perspective of practicing designers. Based on intensive interviews of practitioners, our findings included ten themes organized according to three meta-themes: (a) using theory, (b) struggling with theory, and (c) connections between theory and intuition in craftwork. While these results substantiate (to some degree) the claim that practitioners often find theory too abstract or difficult to apply, they also suggest that practitioners use theory in several important ways and tend to view theory with ambivalence rather than indifference or dislike. Other conclusions regarding the role of theory in design are provided and future directions for theorizing and research are discussed.

Waiti, P. (2005). Evaluation of rural e-Learning in KAWM. Wellington: Ministry of Education. Retrieved from: www.educationcounts.govt.nz/publications/maori_education/5087

Description: Kaupapa Ara Whakawhiti Mātauranga (KAWM) encompassed a number of school improvement initiatives and aimed to:
- improve student achievement;
- improve school performance;
- strengthen school and community relationships;
- upgrade school ICT infrastructure; and
- improve teachers' professional capability through ICT.

Werbach, K. & Hunter, D. (2012). *For the Win. How Game Thinking Can Revolutionize Your Business.* Philadelphia, PA: Wharton Digital Press.

Book Description: Millions flock to their computers, consoles, mobile phones, tablets, and social networks each day to play World of Warcraft, Farmville, Scrabble, and countless other games, generating billions in sales each year. The careful and skillful construction of these games is built on decades of research into human motivation and psychology: A well-designed game goes right to the motivational heart of the human psyche. In For the Win, authors Kevin Werbach and Dan Hunter argue persuasively that gamemakers need not be the only ones benefiting from game design. Werbach and Hunter are lawyers and World of Warcraft players who created the world's first course on gamification at the Wharton School. In their book, they reveal how game thinking – addressing problems like a game designer – can motivate employees and customers and create engaging experiences that can transform your business. For the Win reveals how a wide range of companies are successfully using game thinking. It also offers an explanation of when gamifying makes the most sense and a 6-step framework for using games for marketing, productivity enhancement, innovation, employee motivation, customer engagement, and more.

Whitlock B., & Nanavati, J. (2013). A systematic approach to performative and authentic assessment. *Reference Services Review*, v41, 1, 32-48.

Abstract: *Purpose* – The purpose of this paper is to provide an overview of the learning outcomes assessment process and a five-step, systematic approach for incorporating learning outcomes assessment into information literacy instruction. The paper focuses specifically on using performative and authentic assessments to measure higher-level skills and ensure that students are able to perform the information literacy skills that library instruction programs intend to teach.

Design/methodology/approach – The authors reviewed current assessment literature from both the information literacy and instructional design fields and pulled successful examples from their respective institutions in order to provide an overview of how best to incorporate performative and authentic assessment into the information literacy instruction process. This also includes discussions of assessment terminology, tools, and strategies.

Findings – Engaging in learning outcomes assessment can be invaluable when performed as part of the information literacy instruction process. Following a systematic approach and incorporating tools that allow for performative and authentic assessment will enable librarians to successfully ascertain if students can do what we teach them to do.

Practical implications – This paper provides instruction librarians with a structured way to integrate learning outcomes assessment into their information literacy programs, and it includes an extensive exploration of assessment strategies and tools as they relate to fostering information literacy skills.

Originality/value – There is limited literature on the use of performative and authentic assessment in information literacy instruction. The exploration of a wide selection of possible assessment tools, specifically – their benefits and drawbacks – is especially valuable.

Willis, J. (2009). *The graduate student's handbook*. San José, CA: Psychology Department at San José State University.

<u>Handbook Description</u>: This Handbook provides information about the graduate program and outlines the steps and structure of the I/O Psychology program. The Appendices at the end are important supplemental assessment information and rubrics.

ABOUT THE AUTHOR

Originally from Escanaba, MI, Thomas Buck grew up in Duluth, Minnesota, where he currently resides with his family in an area called Chester Park.

Work for him includes teaching, research, the arts and antiques. With a Ph.D. in Educational Technology / Educational Psychology, an MS in curriculum and Instruction, BA's in History and Philosophy, training and certificates in Education (K-12), Conservation, Restoration and Museumology, and over 25 years teaching experience at the elementary, secondary, post-secondary, undergraduate and graduate levels, Dr. Buck loves learning and the sharing of knowledge.

As a specialist with emphasis in curriculum and instruction, distance learning, behavioral ethics and computer science he is presently an instructor of Computer Science and Ethics at the College of St. Scholastica. He also is conducting an on-going collaborative research project on gender, learning styles and distance learning.

As a cultural entrepreneur and an internationally recognized Conservator of East Asian Historical & Cultural Artifacts, another of Dr. Buck's passions is his research on Japanese and Chinese history, philosophy and fine arts. In addition to his artistic and entrepreneurial ventures in East Asian Arts, he has published a number of related works and books including:

- ❖ Buck, T. L. (2011). *The Art of Tsukamaki*. Lloyd & Tutle Publishing, Ltd.
  ISBN: 987-0984377954

- ❖ Buck, T. L. (2002). *Across the spectrum: Historical trends in Japanese lacquer-ware*. Portland: Lloyd & Tutle Publishing, Ltd.
  ISBN: 0-9843779-1-3

- ❖ Buck, T. L. (1998). *Ancient Japanese Swords and Fittings: A Collection of Restored and Translated Nineteenth Century Woodblock Manuscripts*. Portland: Lloyd & Tutle Publishing, Ltd.
  ISBN: 0-9843779-0-5

Among other things, when not teaching, researching or restoring, Thomas, his wife and son enjoy reading to each other, cycling local trails, down-hill and cross-country skiing, traveling, practicing his Mandarin and learning Hebrew.

Made in the USA
Charleston, SC
14 December 2014